PRAISE FOR THE CFO MYTH

"When I think back to the early days of building my company, I realize how much of my financial learning came through trial and error. Rodrigo's methodology really clicks — it connects the dots in a way that would have saved me a lot of stress and uncertainty. For any founder navigating the numbers for the first time, this book is a thoughtful and practical companion."

—**Marcel Lotufo,** Founder & CEO of Kenoby (acquired by Gupy)

"Rodrigo's CPR methodology has completely transformed how we approach financial decisions at Health Hug. As bootstrapped founders, every dollar counts, and this framework helped us allocate our limited resources with precision, ensuring we built sustainable systems instead of burning through cash on the wrong priorities. This approach got us past MVP and positioned us for real growth. *The CFO Myth* takes bootstrapping to the next level by giving you the financial discipline of a seasoned executive without the overhead. This book is essential reading for any founder who wants to build lean and scale smart."

—**Christina Sloan-Vélez,** Co-founder & Co-CEO, Health Hug

"For founders juggling many hats and family businesses looking to grow responsibly, this book is a lifeline. Rodrigo delivers clear, practical steps to build financial structure without breaking the bank, packed with actionable insights and grounded advice that's perfect for businesses wanting to scale independently."

—**Julio Verdeja,** Operations Manager, Family Owned Boucherie

Also by Rodrigo Rodríguez-Novás

INNOVATE® Miami

https://innovationsoftheworld.com/ecosystems/miami/

https://innovationsoftheworld.com/

THE
CFO
MYTH

TEN REASONS WHY YOU DON'T NEED
A CFO AND FIVE SIGNS YOU DO

THE
CFO
MYTH

RODRIGO RODRÍGUEZ-NOVÁS

NORDES
CONSULTING

NORDES Consulting, LLC
Miami, FL, USA

NORDES Consulting, LLC
Miami, FL, USA

Cataloging-in-Publication Data is on file with the Library of Congress

Paperback ISBN: 979-8-9929616-4-5
Hardcover ISBN: 979-8-9929616-5-2
eBook ISBN: 979-8-9929616-3-8

Book cover and interior design by *the*BookDesigners
Editorial production by KN Literary Arts

www.cfomyth.com

Printed in the United States of America

In Loving Memory
To my father and grandparents, whose wisdom
and love continue to guide me.

In Life
To my mother, for inspiring me to always strive to
become a better version of myself.
To Marcelle, for her endless support and love.
To Sofi and Nico, for being my greatest source of strength,
inspiration, and motivation without even knowing it.

TABLE OF CONTENTS

INTRODUCTION

I watched as he sat at his desk across from mine, face buried in his hands and his shoulders slumped forward in despair. It was 2009 and my coworker was one of the newest casualties of the bank collapse and Great Recession. After working at our bank for over three decades, he had been let go just a few years away from his retirement. To make matters worse, his entire 401(k) retirement had been invested in the company's stock. One stock. A stock that took a sharp dive during the year and reduced his savings for retirement to a small fraction of what they once were. I watched as a lifetime of work left him no better off financially than I was then, in my early twenties. It was heartbreaking to see.

I learned two important lessons that day:

1. I would need to be my own boss if I truly wanted to have the best odds of controlling my future and financial well-being; and
2. I needed to make sure that I was financially savvy and that I educated my family, my future children, and those around me to be financially savvy as well.

The entire situation felt like a verse from a poet who, against their nature, chooses to work in a bank, a vivid image that echoed in my mind during this period. My skills and desires for the future were misaligned with my current position as client manager. I was good at my job, but I didn't love it and often felt underutilized. While grateful for the opportunity and experience, I knew that my future would hold new opportunities for me to use my skills most effectively in the world.

I wish I could go back in time to teach that coworker how to set up his investments and retirement fund to be more resistant to fluctuations in the market and world events. He didn't deserve to spend the later years of his life needing to work and being worried about paying essential bills. Nobody does. But it was only after watching his plight that I was able to reach the conclusion that I am meant to teach as many people as possible to take control of how they earn a living and make smart financial decisions.

THE CFO KNOWLEDGE GAP

A mentor once said to me, "When you're young, work hard for someone else and learn all you can. After a while you'll be ready to work for yourself. If you do things right, then you'll eventually have people who work for you." I took that wisdom to heart. My years of working for one of the largest financial institutions in the world exposed me to different methodologies and best practices in terms of company management and financial knowledge. Eventually I became a consultant and had the opportunity to work with small companies and startups, which led to a great opportunity to serve as a CFO. When that position ended, I decided to go back to helping entrepreneurs and small business owners while launching my own business.

Working with those small businesses, I realized there was a tremendous knowledge gap between what big businesses knew about finances and what small companies had access to—for example, corporations built detailed cash flow forecasts and managed risk proactively, while many small businesses simply hoped sales would cover expenses; large firms had strict internal controls to prevent fraud, whereas entrepreneurs often handled banking, accounting, and spending themselves without oversight, defined processes, and controls. I saw how challenging it was for small businesses to scale and grow with the limited resources available to help them traverse the knowledge gap in a way that was affordable and made sense for the size of their businesses. They knew what skills they needed to hire, but they didn't understand all the ways they could bring those skills in without emptying their bank accounts. I saw firsthand why 20 percent of startups fail within the first year and 65 percent fail within ten years, with the most significant reason for failure being financial issues.[1]

I am also motivated to help those businesses that are already operating but either struggling financially or are slow to grow. I remember a business acquaintance of mine who ran a profitable coffee shop. He had figured out a way to serve an unmet customer need and people were showing up in droves to buy from him. I suggested that if he took care of a few operational issues around supply chain, procedures, and controls, he could easily secure funding or franchise his company and exponentially grow his business.

The thought of scaling seemed to concern him. I understand why he may have been overwhelmed and possibly risk averse to the thought of expanding in a big way. Even a good thing, like having too many customers, creates new problems while also highlighting where the current model isn't working. He eventually did open another location and

---

1 Punjwani, Mehdi. "What Percentage of Startups Fail?" *Forbes*, Forbes Magazine, 23 Oct. 2024, https://www.forbes.com/advisor/business/software/startups-failure-rate.

was unprepared for its success. The information in this book would have given him the additional resources and knowledge to feel confident moving forward, all under the principle of using common sense.

When I was a young kid growing up in Venezuela, my grandparents taught me how to decide if I was using my common sense or not. The first question they told me to ask myself was, "Am I doing something that my grandparents would also choose to do?" If I couldn't see them doing it themselves or wanting me to do it, I probably shouldn't do it. Their second question was, "If I did this, would my parents be happy knowing what I did?" Again, if the answer was "no," then I wasn't using common sense.

The same can apply to your business and the financial decisions you make. I am not saying that you have to spend like my cost-conscious *abuela*, but if you are looking to spend significantly on a certain item or service, you can look to the other businesses of your size to see if they're making similar decisions. If not, you need to ask yourself why you need to be the only one doing it. The second question you could ask yourself with each dollar you spend is, "If my investors knew I was spending on this item, would they approve?" Again, if the answer is "no," why are you using their money this way?

I watched a company with exactly $0 in revenue buy one of the most expensive financial softwares on the market all because they wanted the best and newest program available instead of a simpler, off-the-shelf program available to them for $35 per month. It came as no surprise to me when I heard the business failed; they lost their common sense.

This book is a resource for startups, established small businesses, and family-owned businesses that recognize the need for financial knowledge and support but may not yet know which specific resources or best practices will be most helpful. I want you to know that I'm right there with you—not just offering advice from the sidelines, but living this journey firsthand. I'm applying everything I share here to my own company, which has been in business for just over a year. And yes, the struggle is real. My days are long: building a product and a service, pitching to investors, navigating both fantastic and frustrating vendors, managing limited resources, and balancing cautious optimism with tough, exhausting moments. Every day, I remind myself of our mission and vision—why I'm doing this—and justify the personal sacrifices I make in my own business, including dipping into my own savings, because I believe deeply in what we are building: a company committed to delivering quality healthcare to millions of children and families who desperately need a better system. I could go on—but if you're reading this, I know you already understand. You're living it too.

I want to support businesses so they can grow to the point where they can afford and benefit from the skill set of a full-time CFO. I also want to change the narrative that a CFO *must be* a part of your executive team from the start. Yes, I am saying this as a CFO: You may not need a CFO.

The objective of this book is to provide you (the business owner) with a methodology that will help you leverage the best practices from your industry, structure your business in a way that has better odds for growth, and reframe your perspective on spending, budgets, and what a CFO should be doing for your business. This book has a more accessible price point than private coaching sessions but is just as effective.

Chances are, if you're already starting or running your own company, you're a bright person with brilliant ideas and great potential. Even if you don't have financial knowledge yet, I want you to be aware of all of the things that you can do *without* a CFO. I will also support you to understand when you know the time is right to bring a CFO in, how to ensure you're hiring the right person, and what responsibilities a CFO can take care of at your company. This knowledge can also be translated to other major positions and functional areas. If you can approach hiring and growth with this new framework, you'll have a better chance of setting yourself up for financial success.

The first ten chapters of this book are my reasons why your business doesn't need a full-time CFO at this time. There is a chance that not all of these ten chapters will be applicable to you. While you can easily read this book from cover to cover to get the maximum benefit from it, I also understand that you, an entrepreneur, are most likely short on time. Because of that, the first section can be used like a reference guide in which you only read the chapters that are applicable to you in that moment. Already have a financially responsible business culture? Go ahead and skip that section. Currently making data-driven decisions with good results? You can pass on that chapter, too.

My hope is that this is not a book that you pick up, read once, and then file away on your shelf to collect dust. There are lessons in each chapter that will be relevant to you at different stages of your business. The information most pertinent to you now may change as your company continues to grow and scale. Keep this book within easy reach. Highlight things. Underline. Write notes. The goal is not for you to just read this book—it's for you to *use* it.

The second section of this book contains the five reasons why you might need a full-time CFO. I would recommend reading this entire section at once. If you're very close or at the point where a full-time CFO is right for you, these five chapters build upon each other to get you through scaling and to your company's "exit" from the startup life-cycle. If you are not yet at the point where you're ready for a full-time CFO, these final five chapters will act as a guide to determining where you're heading with your business. They will reassure you that a CFO may not be the person you need to help your business . . . yet. Instead of feeling like you're doing without, you'll be able to see the entire plan and know where you're heading and how to get there. The goal is to be well-timed in bringing on your more expensive resources.

At the end of each chapter you will find recommended activities like how to create a risk matrix and other tools and checklists to take what you've learned and move into action. I highly recommend taking the time to work through each chapter exercise, as they are all highly effective ways to help you get the focus and perspective you need to move your business forward effectively and efficiently. As Benjamin Franklin once said, "An ounce of prevention is worth a pound of cure." Do the work now to save yourself from costly lessons later.

I wish I had had the information contained in this book years ago. I come from a family of immigrants. My grandparents moved from Spain to Venezuela after the Spanish Civil War and re-established their lives and businesses in a new and unknown land. They infused our family with the work ethic that is so commonly found in both immigrant and entrepreneur communities.

Both of my parents inspired my career path. My father started his career working for others and eventually made the shift to entrepreneurship. My mother was a radiologist and split her time between working at one of the top hospitals in the country that was frequented by high-ranking executives and government officials and working in the poorest rural clinics where patients would arrive with bare feet and stab or gunshot wounds. When I was a kid, she would often take me along with her to her job when I wasn't in school. From a young age, I got to see the impact that economic disparities had on people's health and ultimately their lives.

While a career in finance might seem like an unlikely path given my personal mission to help those in need, I see it as a catalyst to help bridge the gap between socioeconomic conditions and access to quality healthcare. I want small businesses to succeed and become big businesses that could help the next small businesses. I want companies to reach a point where they could afford to provide for the health needs of their employees and support their local community. I want adults to become more financially savvy and pass that knowledge on to future generations.

This is a book to improve the health of your business, and I hope it also becomes a movement to improve the health and well-being of our world. Thank you for being a part of it.

PART I

▼

WHY YOU DON'T NEED A CFO

CHAPTER 1

YOU'RE NOT READY TO LISTEN

There's so much to do as the founder or CEO of a new business. You're often one of the few individuals who hold the vision, mission, and know-how to get started on a journey that I've always found to be incredibly rewarding. Starting a new business ignites a feeling in me that I never felt from my many years working for someone else. I imagine that if you're reading this book, you may feel the same—your own passion for innovating and creating, impacting and disrupting drives you to pour your heart into your work.

Even if you've had your business for a while or have inherited a family business, being in charge means always looking for new ways to grow and evolve, meet the needs of your customers, efficiently manage your costs, and stay relevant to technology and cultural changes. Perhaps entrepreneurs are wired differently than other people. What is it that drives you to do what you do? How does your vision for your life fit with your vision for your business and the way you work?

One of the most useful tools to have as an entrepreneur is introspection. You have to have a realistic idea of where you excel and where your blind spots are. Entrepreneurs must have a do-it-yourself attitude when starting a business as well as pragmatism to closely monitor every dollar they spend along the way. Oftentimes you know the type of help you need, but you're not sure when you need it or how to afford it.

Financial guidance is generally high on that list of entrepreneurial needs, but that doesn't mean you need to hire a financial professional from day one. In fact, that's what this first chapter is all about: identifying why your business might not be ready for a CFO and how to know when it is. Through my work experience, both in my own business and as a CFO for other companies, I've found that a company is not at all ready to bring in a CFO if it's not ready to listen.

You may be thinking to yourself, "Who in their right mind would bring in an expensive role, like a CFO, and then *not* listen to them?" I've found there are three primary reasons why business owners are not ready to listen to a CFO. Sometimes it's not a matter of not *wanting* to listen; it's the fact that they simply can't. The timing isn't right.

As you go through this chapter, I encourage you to use your introspective skills to be honest about where you and your business are in terms of both business needs and leadership mentality. If you can do that, you will save yourself tremendous amounts of money by not bringing in the wrong person at the wrong time.

People are often taken aback when I suggest that they're not ready to listen to a CFO. Perhaps their minds go to thoughts of an obstinate teenager who knows better and chooses not to listen, such as refusing advice on managing money or ignoring guidance about long-term planning.

While that may be part of the story, there are other very valid reasons why you are not ready to listen to a CFO, and they have little to do with you.

Reason 1: Your Business Is Not at the Right Developmental Stage
Do you have a brand-new business or concept of a business? What do you think is the most important thing you need to be focused on right now? I can say with certainty that it is not your financial ratios. In fact, you may be so early on in your business creation journey that you have little to no financial data to even work with. At this point your focus is on building your idea and getting it off the ground.

In the earliest stages of business, the majority of your time, energy, and resources need to be focused on getting clear on the vision of your business and how you're going to get to that first sale. That's it. You'll need to focus on building your business idea and developing it. You may need to build a prototype to see if your idea is possible. You may also shift to create your minimal viable product (MVP) so that you can get feedback from your potential customers before investing more money into development.

You may not be ready to listen to a CFO if your business is in the stage where you're still looking for your first clients and learning how to market and sell your idea. You are still in the stage of clarifying who you want and need to be in the market in order for your business to be profitable. If you consider your business to be disruptive to the industry you're entering, this stage may take even longer because you're charting a path into a greater unknown.

If you are in the stage where your primary need is to get your idea off the ground, then you are not ready to listen to a CFO. Why is that? Because chances are, whatever the CFO says (or whatever you want the CFO to say) has little to do with getting your business up and running. I'm not saying that we don't need to be mindful of expenses right from the start. (In later chapters I'll talk about the importance of budgeting, establishing a financially responsible business culture, and knowing your numbers.) But at this stage, financial planning is not the number-one priority on your list.

There are three recommendations I have for startups considering whether or not the time is right to bring in a full-time CFO:

1. **Determine if you have a product-market fit** – Product-market fit means that you have a product or service, you've established that there is a market of customers who have a need for your product or service, and you've determined that what you're offering is actually a good fit for those customers' needs. Do not waste your time rushing wildly into entrepreneurship just because you have an idea that you want to be a business. Establish your viability first before you consider bringing in your full executive team

2. **Determine if you have controls for growth in place** – Depending on your business, it may be a very quick ramp-up for growth. Before you bring in a CFO, ensure that you have spent time thinking through your plan for growth and the controls you will need to have in place to meet those growth needs. Controls should be around spending allowances and approvals, hiring and onboarding, quality control, data access, and anything else of special importance to your business. While a full-time CFO can help you with structuring controls, this is something that you can (and should) do *before* you bring them in

3. **Determine if you've generated sufficient revenue to support your hiring** – If you don't have the right funding or revenue streams, you are not ready to bring in a CFO. Your focus needs to be on generating clients and getting your product or service to market before you bring in this expensive organizational role

I have encountered businesses that attempt to bring in a full-time CFO from the start of the business simply because that feels like something they're supposed to do. They request budgets, they ask for reports and forms, and they can brag to their friends that they "have to talk to their CFO" so that their new business feels more legitimate. But a founder will have more important areas to focus on and lacks the time and energy to work in partnership with their full-time CFO.

Unless the CFO is the co-founder of the business, they're often relegated to tasks like making sure tax paperwork is properly filed, accounts are reconciled, and financial reports are generated. The role of CFO should be so much more than that. Until you've established that you have a viable product-market fit and a plan for growth, you're not at the right developmental stage to get the most out of hiring a full-time CFO.

Reason 2: You Don't Have Time

Sometimes not listening to your CFO or other members of your leadership team is not a matter of not wanting to listen. I know many company founders who would have loved to have a knowledgeable CFO to help with some of their decision-making. Most often, founders and CEOs lack the time to engage deeply with a CFO, even when one is available, as they dedicate roughly 61 percent of their time to meetings and a significant portion to email correspondence, according to a study of CEO time allocation.[1]

In the early days of a company, speed and agility are everything. While there is value in the advice of an experienced CFO, most business leaders do not have the ability to be slowed down in the decision-making process. These early days often include heavier overhead costs and immense pressure to bring that first dollar through the door. You are not looking strategically into the distant future. You are in a tactical, boots-on-the-ground hustle to bring a concept to fruition. Save the advanced strategic plan with a CFO for the future. Right now there is no time.

Bringing in a CFO (or any employee, for that matter) takes time to get them up to speed, especially if you're a new company without all of your policies and procedures in place. Because of this, many company leaders believe that they can work faster by doing things themselves rather than teaching another person how to do it. They may have the feeling that bringing in a CFO will create a burdensome weight on their shoulders. And that may be a correct assumption.

A CFO is an asset to your company, but their abilities may be limited based on the amount of information provided to them. If you do not have time to spend with your CFO right now, then hold off on this role. There will come a day when your business

---

1   Michael E. Porter and Nitin Nohria, "How CEOs Manage Time," *Harvard Business Review* 96, no. 4 (July–August 2018): 42–51.
https://hbr.org/2018/07/how-ceos-manage-time

needs to grow and the knowledge of a CFO will become even more important than the knowledge of the founder. But that may not be the case today.

Reason 3: Your Ego Gets in the Way
Want to threaten your company's health and make life harder on yourself for the foreseeable future? Act like you know more than anyone else in the world! I have seen this attitude sink more businesses than I can share. The scrappy DIY-type personality that can help start a business also has the potential negative side effect of being a controlling micromanager.

Creating an idea and bringing it to life through a successful business is both impressive and admirable. Unfortunately, there are leaders that let this go to their heads . . . sometimes even before they've created a company to truly be impressed with. They bring in a team, but care more about showing off to their team than taking that team's advice. Perhaps you've worked somewhere where the boss had a "my way or the highway" approach and steamrolled your ideas. It's not a great environment to work in and if you are that type of boss, then you are absolutely going to waste your money by bringing in a CFO or any other expert.

I was once hired by a company that was scaling quickly. I had a good relationship with the founder and I knew he trusted me and the work I did. He also loved to be the good guy and the one who other employees revered. Very early on I realized it was a regular practice of his to either debate the advice and recommendations I was giving, or he would listen to them and then go off and do his own thing.

This mentality worked for a while. He was a smart guy and had successfully started a business with a solid product-market fit. But what worked when his company was small wasn't necessarily what worked as he moved through a growth phase. I remember one day he approached me to say he wanted to increase everyone's salary at the company by a certain percentage.

While this may seem like a noble thing to do, it was not grounded in any data or strategic decision-making. I reminded him that the company already offered a competitive salary that was above average for the area and had a generous benefits package. Most importantly, I cautioned him that this decision would have long-term financial implications that the company would potentially not be able to support.

I'm not sure what exactly prompted him to desire this company-wide pay increase. Perhaps he read a news story about some other company in some other part of the world that did it and had soaring productivity. Perhaps his ego stepped in and he wanted to play Robin Hood for the entire team. He ignored my advice and went ahead with the raises. What was a short-term joy for the employees ended up being a long-term pain as they lost their jobs and the company went out of business. Had he listened to the expert and data-driven advice he was given, he would have directed his money and energy to a problem at the company that actually needed fixing. Pay rates were not an issue. This decision cost everyone in the end.

We can all benefit from self-awareness and identifying when our ego gets in the way of listening to others and making the right decisions rather than the fun, easy, or flashy decisions. If you are not willing to put your ego to the side, then you are not ready to bring on an executive team and benefit from their knowledge. This doesn't just apply to bringing in a CFO—it's relevant to every single functional area where you would bring in a leader or leadership team. Do not bring in a team that will only tell you what you want to hear. Also, do not bring in a team if you're not willing to listen to the good, the bad, and the ugly of what they have to tell you about your business. You'll be wasting their time and your money.

WHEN SPEED IS THE PRIORITY

When starting a business, each day that passes until you get to your first sale is money out the door. There is an absolute need and pressure to get your product or service to market as quickly and efficiently as possible. In the next chapter we'll be discussing my proprietary core-priorities-resources (CPR) approach to starting and running a business with a lean-spending and agile mindset.

At this stage, opportunities appear and disappear overnight, competitors move faster than you can plan, and the businesses that succeed are the ones that act decisively—not the ones that overanalyze. You may find yourself needing to make decisions with 70 percent of the information, trusting your instincts, and focusing on momentum over perfection. Having an organization that is top-heavy in management or includes an unnecessary role like a full-time CFO will slow you down and be more expensive. Now is not the time for bureaucracy or labored decision-making (though we'd also like to try and avoid those as much as possible in the future as well).

Instead, I suggest looking to people who you have on your team already who may also possess skills in other areas. You may have hired someone to help with product design without realizing that they also have their MBA and may have sufficient financial knowledge to help you structure the company as well. This phase is a time for pooling the skills and resources of the people you already have and figuring out how to make them work as quickly and cost-effectively as possible. Eventually, you will have the time to listen. Now is simply not the time, and you're not ready for a full-time CFO.

USE THE OCEAN MODEL TO BUILD YOUR CEO SELF-AWARENESS

Personality tests are great ways that you can grow your self-awareness as a leader.

Research by psychologists Robert McCrae, Paul Costa, and Lewis Goldberg has shown that the Big Five personality traits often referred to as the acronyms OCEAN or CANOE are consistent over time, across cultures and situations, making them one of the most scientifically validated frameworks for understanding human personality.

This framework helps individuals and businesses understand work styles, leadership potential, and decision-making abilities. It measures individuals across five key dimensions:

1. **Openness** – Creativity, curiosity, and willingness to try new experiences
2. **Conscientiousness** – Organization, discipline, and goal-directed behavior
3. **Extraversion** – Sociability, energy, and enthusiasm in social interactions
4. **Agreeableness** – Compassion, cooperation, and consideration for others
5. **Neuroticism** – Emotional stability and ability to handle stress

Benefits of the Big Five Model:

1. **Scientific validity** – Backed by extensive psychological research

2. **Practical insights** – Helps individuals and businesses understand work styles, leadership potential, and team dynamics
3. **Flexible application** – Used in hiring, self-improvement, leadership development, and relationship insights

By measuring openness, conscientiousness, extraversion, agreeableness, and neuroticism, it provides deep insights into behavior and how to optimize performance in professional and personal life.

Personality tests like the Big Five help support you in identifying the best type of people to work with you on your business journey (as well as in your personal life). In the case where maybe a person's personality doesn't seem like a great fit but they have the specific skill set you need to hire, a personality test can also teach you the best styles and techniques to work effectively with that employee. I strongly recommend taking a few minutes out of your day to complete the following assessment before you go on to later chapters.

INSTRUCTIONS

Rate each statement below based on your leadership tendencies using the following scale:

1 = Strongly Disagree, 2 = Disagree, 3 = Neutral,
4 = Agree, 5 = Strongly Agree

Provide a brief example from your leadership experience to support your rating.

1. **Openness** – I am comfortable embracing change, innovation, and risk-taking in my leadership role
   Rating: [ ] 1 [ ] 2 [ ] 3 [ ] 4 [ ] 5
   Example from my leadership experience:

   _____

2. **Conscientiousness** – I am highly disciplined, organized, and goal-oriented in my daily work as a leader
   Rating: [ ] 1 [ ] 2 [ ] 3 [ ] 4 [ ] 5
   Example from my leadership experience:

   _____

3. **Extraversion** – I feel energized by networking, meetings, and team interactions in my leadership role
   Rating: [ ] 1 [ ] 2 [ ] 3 [ ] 4 [ ] 5
   Example from my leadership experience:

   _____

4. **Agreeableness** – I naturally collaborate, empathize, and seek consensus when leading others
   Rating: [ ] 1 [ ] 2 [ ] 3 [ ] 4 [ ] 5

Example from my leadership experience:

_____

5. **Neuroticism** –I effectively handle stress, setbacks, and emotional pressure as a leader
   Rating: [ ] 1 [ ] 2 [ ] 3 [ ] 4 [ ] 5
   Example from my leadership experience:

_____

6. **Reflection** – I have a clear strength in one of the Big Five traits that I can leverage to improve my leadership
   Rating: [ ] 1 [ ] 2 [ ] 3 [ ] 4 [ ] 5
   Which trait and how will you leverage it?

_____

7. I am aware of a potential blind spot in one of the Big Five traits that may hinder my leadership
   Rating: [ ] 1 [ ] 2 [ ] 3 [ ] 4 [ ] 5
   Which trait and what will you watch for?

_____

8. I am committed to taking a specific action step in the next 30 days to enhance my leadership based on this assessment
   Rating: [ ] 1 [ ] 2 [ ] 3 [ ] 4 [ ] 5
   What is your action step?

_____

SCORING AND INTERPRETATION

1. Assign points based on your ratings (1 for Strongly Disagree, 2 for Disagree, etc.) for statements 1–5, which correspond to the Big Five traits

2. Sum these points for a total score (5–25)

3. Higher scores (4–5 per trait) indicate strengths: High Openness suggests adaptability and innovation; high Conscientiousness reflects organization and reliability; high Extraversion indicates energy from social interactions; high Agreeableness shows collaboration and empathy; and high Neuroticism (reverse-scored, so 1 is better) suggests emotional resilience

4. Lower scores (1–2) highlight areas for growth

5. For statements 6–8, ratings reflect confidence in leveraging strengths, awareness of blind spots, and commitment to action

6. Use your total score and individual ratings to identify traits to enhance or balance in your leadership practice

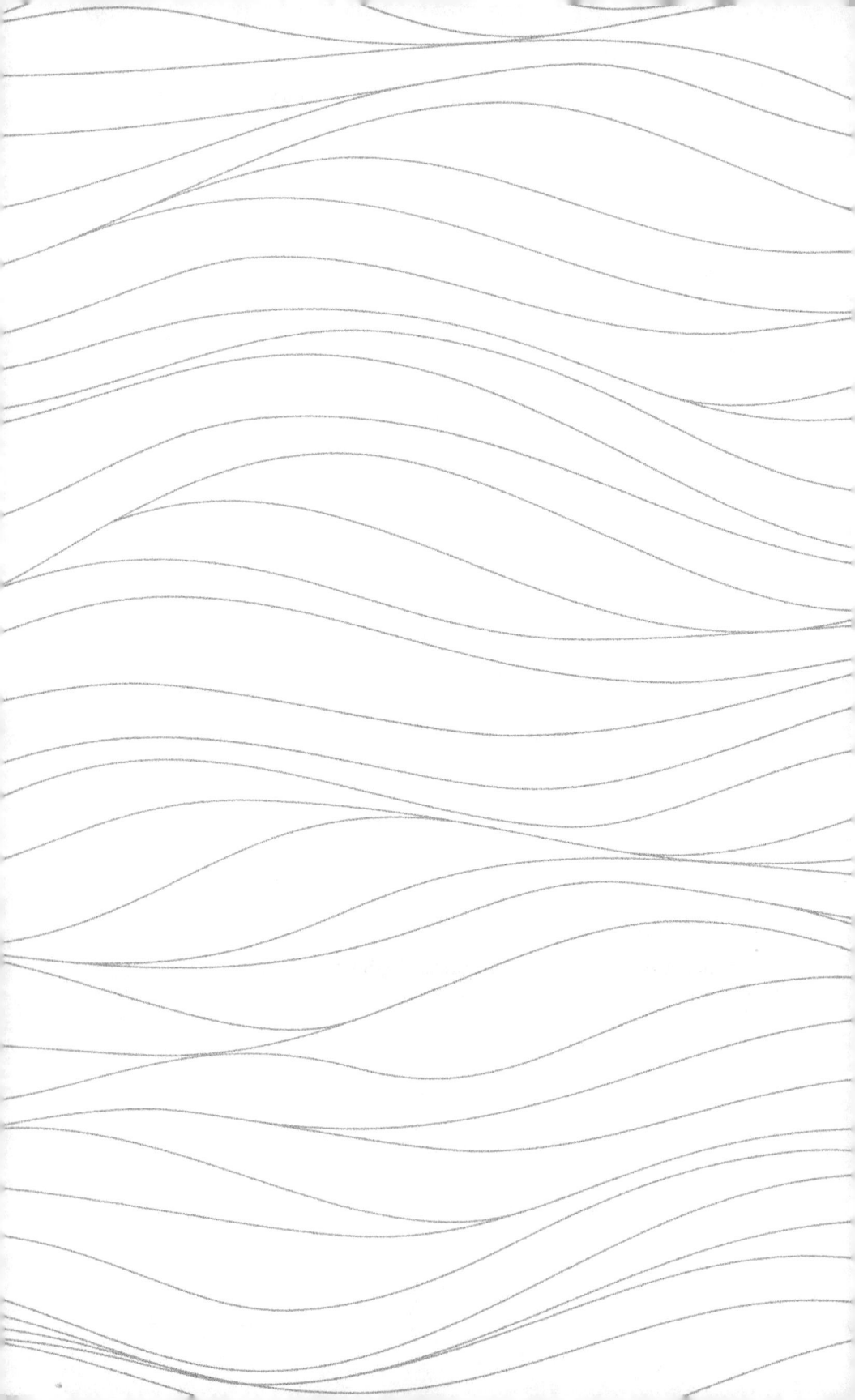

CHAPTER 2

YOU HAVE IMPLEMENTED
A CPR APPROACH

What separates the living from the dead? I don't mean this in a phil-osophical sense, like having a sense of purpose or a "why" for start-ing your day. I'm sure there are any number of sarcastic answers one could come up with as well, like your ability to escape the confines of grey cubicle walls to fulfill your dreams as a Highland cow farmer. For this moment, let's look at this from a purely physical sense. What is the most basic physiological function that separates those who are alive from those who are not?

According to the legal definition in the US, there are two ways in which a body is defined as dead. Cardiopulmonary death is the irre-versible cessation of the heartbeat. Brain death is the irreversible ces-sation of certain brain activity. For the sake of this metaphor, we're going to think about cardiopulmonary death. If we have a body without a heartbeat, we don't have life.

Now let's say we want to take that body to a gym to do twenty pushups or train for a 5k race. I know what you may be thinking now: "Rodrigo, have you lost your mind? Why would you take a body without a heartbeat and think you could even start to train it for a 5k?!"

It seems crazy, right? Not only is it crazy, but it will be a fruitless attempt. It doesn't matter how many goals you set, what kind of nutrition program you have set up, or the quality of coaches you have. You can surround the body with words of affirmation, incentive plans, and project management boards. If there is no heartbeat, then nothing is going to happen.

Why have I painted this outlandish example for you? Because what is easy to see when it comes to human life becomes more of a challenge to see when it comes to the life of a business. Sadly, I have witnessed my fair share of examples of people starting new businesses but ignoring the heartbeat. There is an undeniable excitement from founders for the future vision of what the business could grow to be. However, inexperienced owners may lose sight of what the first steps are that matter most. If the business never gets its heart beating strongly, then it's not going to accomplish any of the things its team sets out to do.

What exactly is the heartbeat of a company? Your business's heartbeat is the solution to whatever market problem you're trying to solve. It's the niche thing you offer to get your first dollars of revenue through the door. That revenue can then start to become the lifeblood of your business.

If you look at our business from the standpoint of identifying its critical function—the heartbeat of your business—you become more capable of understanding what your business actually needs to live and what fluff exists in your operations. This perspective is what led me to develop the CPR methodology for keeping your business alive. Like cardiopulmonary resuscitation, this business CPR model focuses on the most critical component of your business and what determines if your business is alive or dead.

THE CPR METHODOLOGY

CPR stands for core, priorities, and resources. It is a lean approach to bringing your business to life and increasing its chances of reaching its full potential. If you already have an established business, you can still use the core-priority-resources methodology to analyze how you are running things. In fact, using the CPR method may help you recognize if you've taken your attention away from the critical heartbeat function of your business and could explain why you haven't been able to optimize your performance.

What I love about this methodology is that it's not complicated and can be translated to virtually any type of industry or size of company. It's about working smart and focusing your efforts so that you can grow and scale sustainably while never losing sight of your heartbeat.

There are three steps to the CPR methodology:
1. **Define your core** – The solution that you're providing to solve a problem
2. **Identify your priorities** – What you need to do to follow best practices and create operational efficiencies
3. **Allocate your resources** – Who and what you need to bring in in the order of criticality

If you're in the startup phase of your business, it is absolutely essential that you devote time on the front end to identifying your CPR. Doing so will ensure that you are more efficient in your project management as you develop the business.

This is also a beneficial exercise for already established businesses. It is worth your time to step back and critically consider your CPR and if your current operations align with it. There are clear opportunities for improvement in any areas where the two don't match up. It may open your eyes to potential pivots you need to make to streamline and strengthen your core.

CORE

In the core, your goal is to identify what your primary business function is and how you can allocate resources to that function. It means discerning between what you absolutely need to bring those first dollars of revenue through the door and what counts as a miscellaneous cost, like unnecessary travel if you can conduct business over a video conference or giving company cell phones to your employees that don't need one to perform their job.

Take this, for example: If you are a coffee shop, then your core business is that cup of coffee that can be served to customers. If you are a company that is helping others learn a new language, your core may be the app you create for customers to learn, practice, and track their progress. How do we know these things are our core? Because without that cup of coffee or language app, you are simply a concept of a business.

Identifying your core means getting clear on your MVP (minimum viable product). Your MVP is the most basic version of your product or service that includes the features needed to make it usable or sellable but no more. Creating your MVP allows you to test the most important features of what you offer to ensure that they work and establish that there is a market need for what you're offering. The MVP of that coffee shop is that really good cup of coffee, not the full menu of 57 coffee options plus pastries and free Wi-Fi while you sip. For the language company, the MVP is the app that provides enough functionality for a person to learn the language, but without additional functionalities like live tutoring options with a native speaker. It may also mean starting with one language, or just a few, rather than a full catalog that includes Hawaiian and Yiddish.

The goal of using the MVP approach to determine your core product or service is to gain maximum information from your customers with the least amount of investment possible. It provides you with the make-or-break feedback to know if your business is worth pursuing. It will also help you identify if you need to go back to the drawing board or if the business concept should be scratched entirely. While this may be a hard pill to swallow, it's far better to have this information before you've invested all of your money or filled warehouses with inventory.

It is worth noting that you may find yourself needing to pivot. That is okay (and sometimes absolutely necessary), but it doesn't mean that you should lose sight of your core business. There may even be pivots that require the core of your business to change, like if you develop one product, but customer feedback or potential clients are asking for a different product that will help you earn revenue faster.

PRIORITIES

Once you've identified the core of your business, it's time to identify your key priorities. These priorities are the things you need to do in order to bring your core to life, and the ideal way to execute them is by following industry best practices and creating operational efficiencies. This is where you separate the "need to have" from the "neat to have" to get established. Utilizing the skills and services a CFO has to offer will serve you at some point. Chances are, for most new businesses, you do not need a CFO to create your MVP or start to earn revenue.

Depending on the complexity of your business, establishing your priorities might be as simple as creating a list of everything that needs to be done and ranking the items by criticality and operational order. Some things must be done before others, by certain deadlines, or with enough lead time to allow for required inspections and approvals.

Identifying and ordering your business priorities will provide you with an excellent experience to learn what your business needs to survive before starting any additional workflows.

RESOURCES

In the CPR approach, your resources are the necessary things that you need in order for the heart of the business to beat. If your priorities list was *what* you needed to do, your resource list are your things that explain *how* you'll do it. These are the people and things you will need for your business in the initial and future stages in order to operate.

1. **Start by making a list of who the people most important to your business are and what kind of things you'll need** – There are some things that every business needs, like a bank account to receive cash and make payments, a basic accounting system to record transactions, and legal support for establishing your business paperwork and filing. There may also be things that are either specific to your industry or level of expertise.

2. **Identify which of your resources you may be able to outsource** – Evaluate whether outsourcing makes sense based on your current capacity needs. For example, if there is a tech component to your business, it may make more sense to outsource the need as you work to create and refine your MVP rather than hiring an employee. Often this determination is best made by evaluating the workload. If you don't have enough work to fill an employee's capacity full-time, then outsourcing is often the right choice.

3. **Determine the order of criticality** – This can be a challenge for business owners who feel like they need *everything* to get started. Pretend you have half the budget to spend. Who or what must you have on board before the other things? What things could your business not survive without? It's amazing what incredible insights and work-arounds business owners can find when they're forced to look at their needs with a critical lens.

4. **Do not hire anyone before you're ready to fully utilize them** – If you don't have enough work for them, see if there is a way that you can contract them for partial hours or hold off on hiring them until you have more work. You can also

inquire what other skills they have that you can use in other areas of your business until there is enough work for their primary role (e.g., have a marketing person who minored in accounting and can help with bookkeeping tasks).

For startups, the CPR methodology dictates that you only hire or acquire things if they meet the following criteria:

1. You can afford them
2. The heartbeat of the business cannot survive without them
3. They will support you getting to your MVP

While CPR is about helping you move more expediently to market, it's also about taking the time to slow down and do things the right way rather than cutting corners and expecting to fix things later.

CPR METHODOLOGY EXAMPLE

I am currently in the process of launching a new startup in the healthcare tech sector and have been using the CPR approach with my co-founder and team to ensure we are working methodically and in stages, never losing sight of the heartbeat of our business and what we set out to do. Improving healthcare for others has always been a mission of mine. My co-founder is also passionate about this work and has extensive experience working with physicians as well as patients and their families. Together we created a vision for what we wanted this business to be and identified the current issues in healthcare it could solve. But the vision was broad and long-term. We knew that if we wanted to get there, we would have to niche down and get really good at a small sector of the market. We chose pediatrics.

Through our research, we identified that focusing on pediatrics would allow us to make the biggest impact in a short amount of time. We found that pediatricians faced capacity issues and that many children in the US don't even have a pediatrician assigned to them and instead see a primary care physician. There are real issues with the quality of care that the current market capacity is able to provide. We are ready to make a difference!

We used the CPR methodology to get clear on the basics of our business. We know what we want to do, now we need to answer:

1. How will we do it?
2. Where will we get funding?
3. How will we pay our bills?
4. Who or what do we need to help us bring in our first client?

When it comes to our core, we must initially focus our energy on creating a technology platform to support providers and caregivers in order to improve patient outcomes, the quality of care, and their overall experience. This means our priority for allocating our resources is having someone design the technology for what we are trying to accomplish. While at some point we will need a full-time tech person (and eventually a full tech team), for now it makes the most sense to outsource the technology piece to a UX/UI (user experience/user interface) designer with a "scope of work" contract.

I remember watching an interview with Steve Jobs, founder of Apple, who said that his philosophy in technology was to start with the customer experience and work backward from there, rather than design technology first and figure out who to sell it to. To get this much-needed feedback from the industry, we formed an advisory committee that has shared valuable expertise on what barriers physicians, patients, and caregivers are currently facing that our technology could help to solve. Creating an advisory board made up of people who would potentially be our future product users and paying them at an hourly rate for their feedback allows us to minimize our spending while ensuring that we're creating a product that the market needs.

I know that at some point we will need a sales and marketing team to help us connect with potential customers. We'll need an HR manager once we have more employees. We'll need various levels of accounting and financial support depending on our size and complexity. But for right now, we are a technology company and need to make sure that the heartbeat of tech gets first priority.

CPR LESSONS

There are a few guideposts as you implement the CPR methodology into your business. If you are unsure as to whether something is part of the core of your business, a priority, or a necessary resource, these might help you to determine the right course of action.

1. **Put your money where your money is going to come from** – Focus the majority of your funds in the startup phase on whatever your future source of revenue is. This may mean that you as the CEO or founder will have to wear many hats and maybe not take a payment from the business until you've developed

something that is generating money for the business. Spend money on what will get you to your MVP, while also remembering that the "M" in MVP stands for "minimum."

2. **Don't spend a dollar you don't need to spend** – The CPR methodology helps you approach your business with a smart financial mindset and avoid sending a single dollar out the door that doesn't need to be spent. Most startups have investors, whether family and friends or unrelated parties. You have a duty to make sure that you are spending on things that are reasonable and that your investors would approve of, like a moderately priced hotel to attend that trade show rather than luxury accommodations. Keep in mind that your investors may not understand all of the "whys" behind your spending, but you need to make all decisions in the best financial interest of the company.

3. **Bring in more as you can afford and need it** – The CPR methodology is built around simplicity. I have found a lot of inspiration from observing other businesses and ways to do things that are outside the conventional approach. I remember an interview with Apple's CFO, Luca Maestri, in which he shared that he manages Apple's $230B of cash with a team of only seven people. His team is a sliver of the size most other companies have compared to the size of the asset being managed. According to Maestri, though, "If you have the right people, you don't need a lot of them."

Implementing the CPR approach in your own business may be exactly the reason why you do not need a CFO yet. A CFO is an expensive resource who will eventually be a valuable strategic asset when the time is right. A CFO, however, is unlikely to provide a direct benefit to getting you to your MVP (unless he or she is a co-founder). If you're like most startups, the cost of hiring a CFO is not money you need to be spending at this time and is likely outside of your current budget. You'll get there eventually!

If you are operating in a lean way, a CFO should not be a part of your initial leadership team (unless they also happen to be one of your co-founders). A CFO brings strategic experience that is beneficial for analyzing your business across departments or planning for future growth, but they aren't a key component of helping you reach your MVP.

Some people conflate handling money in their business with the need to have a CFO. It's important to understand that if you are truly operating using the CPR methodology, then it's unlikely that a CFO should be a part of your plan.

The CPR methodology is about bringing common-sense decision-making back to business. It's about getting clear and being honest with ourselves about what is a business *need* versus a business *want*. It's about staying focused on getting to our MVP and getting those first revenue dollars through the door as quickly as possible. While my personal philosophy is that companies should always operate with a lean financial mindset, the startup phase is absolutely the time when you need to be the most stringent with your spending. In doing so, you're setting yourself up for a greater shot at future success.

Remember, there is no way to enter the race if you don't have a heart that is beating.

TOOTH-TO-TAIL APPROACH TO RESOURCE ALLOCATION

One of the most important skills for developing and running a successful organization is learning how to do more with less. Across the years and many unique business opportunities I've been a part of, I've had the opportunity to learn various techniques that strategically evaluate a company's operations. The one I'll share with you now comes from a great manager that I worked for while supporting a Chief Information Officer at a large organization. He introduced me to a military approach to efficiency known as a Tooth-to-Tail Ratio (T3R).

In a military context, T3R is the ratio of how many military personnel (tail) it takes to support each combat soldier (tooth). For a business, the T3R looks at your ratio of back-end support (tail) to the people on the front line working directly with your customers (tooth). Determining your optimal ratio will help you to manage resources as you grow and scale.

Consider this: You have a salesperson who will bring in 100 patients for your medical business. For each 100 patients, you'll also need one nurse and one customer service representative. Your driver for figuring out the ratio of support is your number of customer service reps and the amount of patients they bring in. Hypothetically, for every 100 patients that your salesperson brings to your business, you will trigger the hiring of an additional nurse and customer service representative. This creates a simple algorithm to figure out how to scale the size of your team based on your revenue driver without eroding your profit margins by hiring resources before you need them.

To implement T3R in your business:

1. **Look at each function in your business and determine what the driver is for that role** – If you have a restaurant, what is the driver for the number of waitstaff or cooks you need? If you offer credit cards, how many customers can each agent handle in call volume?

2. **Determine if this ratio is sustainable** – For the revenue that you bring in from each "tooth," can you support the cost of the "tail"? If you have too high of a ratio, this may mean that you're operating inefficiently and need to look for ways to automate or streamline. If your ratio is too low, your frontline employees may be overworked.

3. **Plan your future resource needs accordingly** – Once you've identified your ideal ratio, you will have a clearer picture of who you need to hire and when.

There is no one-size-fits-all ratio for businesses. Your optimal ratio will depend on the size of your business, your industry, and your business model. Small companies will generally have a lower T3R ratio to remain agile and save on costs. Large companies may have a higher T3R due to the complexity of their operations.

CHAPTER 3

YOU NEED AN ACCOUNTING EXPERT, NOT A FINANCIAL EXPERT

Accounting is not finance and finance is not accounting. Claiming they're one and the same is akin to saying knitting is crocheting because they both involve tools and produce a woven textile. Or that soft, salty queso fresco and pungent, creamy blue cheese are interchangeable in dishes because they're both cheese.

There is absolutely overlap between accounting and finance and often they're combined into the same department (usually the finance department of an organization) because they both involve money and numbers. Nevertheless, their intentions and purposes are very different. If you are clear that you understand the difference, then you can move on from this chapter. But if you find yourself commingling the roles of accounting and finance when you look at your own business, then I encourage you to really focus here because it's an important distinction that might save you a lot of money early on.

If you have a solid accounting foundation in your business and you're not in the growth stages, then you do not need a CFO. Let's take a look at what accounting does versus finance to paint a clearer picture of why a CFO is most likely unnecessary if your accounting is in order.

THE PURPOSE OF ACCOUNTING

Accounting is a necessity for every single business. It is one of the first pieces that must be established at the formation of the business because you need it to handle the primary purpose of your business: managing the flow of money. I look at the function of accounting as more than just debits and credits. How you account for your money is also tied to things like setting up a bank account and potentially having a corporate credit card. Accounting is about recording what is going in and out, reconciling against what your bank and credit card statements say happened, monitoring your spending and your revenue, and knowing what you still owe and what money you expect to come in (accounts payable and accounts receivable).

Accounting is based at a point in time and looks backward, recording and reporting on things that have already happened. I consider it to be factual reporting because it should have evidence to support each transaction, whether through receipts, physical inventory, or contract agreements. Accounting often uses a short-term lens of one year or less to see what we've spent and what revenue we've generated, though we may also do year-over-year comparisons to notice seasonal trends or the impact of new policies or operational changes.

Accounting is so vital to an organization because it is a significant part of compliance. Regardless of the country you operate in, you have to report on the operation of your business. You have to pay some form of taxes, or file a report demonstrating if and why you don't owe taxes. Your accounting needs to be up to date, accurate, and verifiable if and when you're audited. Eventually, as your business grows and you seek more savvy investors or do an IPO, your accounting and financial statements will be a key part of any due diligence process to raise additional capital or execute on your exit strategy.

THE PURPOSE OF FINANCE

Finance is related to accounting but has an entirely different goal. While accounting is the record of what has happened, finance is most often a future projection of what's to come. Accounting looks backward at the year. Finance looks forward ten years. Accounting is looking at what is. Finance is looking at what could be. It's strategic and is the role or department that is used to steer the company into the future.

Isn't that the job of the CEO? Partially. A CEO is the visionary of the company who sees where things are and plots a course of action forward to where they want the company to be in the future. The role of a CFO is to act as the right-hand advisor of the CEO and connect the dots internally in the business to support the plan for growth. If the CEO determines the "what" of goals, the CFO determines the "how."

While the function of accounting is valuable to the company, it's the role of finance to add value to the company by determining better ways to raise capital, manage risk, work with investors, optimize cash flow and operating margins, and more. While a CFO must have a knowledge of accounting, they do not have to be an accountant or a CPA. There is a reason why accounting and finance are separate majors or concentrations in college; the content is not the same. Someone with a background in finance or economics may be better qualified for the role of CFO than someone with an accounting degree. More important than their specific degree, you want a CFO who has broad experience working with multiple departments and the ability to connect the dots within your business. A CPA may make an excellent CFO if they are able to step into the role of visionary.

UNDERSTANDING ACCOUNTING ROLES

Because your CFO does not necessarily need to be an accountant, I think it's important to spend some time talking about what certain accounting roles are and what your expectations should be for those positions. Understand that accounting is a technical resource and you will want someone who knows their stuff when it comes to properly recording transactions, managing documentation for audits, preparing reports, and filing taxes.

Bookkeeper

A bookkeeper is responsible for handling the day-to-day transactions of a business and recording them in the general ledger. They make journal entries related to income, expenses, and payments; manage accounts payable and accounts receivable; and may reconcile bank and credit card statements. Their goal is to maintain accurate financial records in your accounting software. Some bookkeepers may also be able to assist with payroll processing. A bookkeeper is generally not involved in financial strategy or advanced reporting.

Senior Accountant

A senior accountant is responsible for the integrity of financial data and the preparation of more advanced financial reports. In addition to preparing the balance sheet and income statement, they may ana-lyze financial data for accuracy and trends. Your senior accountant should be able to manage your business tax filings and ensure com-pliance with financial reporting regulations. They often oversee the work of bookkeepers and review entries for accuracy.

A senior accountant may provide insights on budgeting, forecasting, and financial planning depending on their experience. During an audit, your senior accountant is often the one who will liaise with external auditors and assist with providing documentation. They act as a bridge between your day-to-day bookkeeping and high-level oversight, which may be a controller, CEO, or some other position depending on your business setup.

Controller
Controllers are often the highest level companies hire within the accounting function. They are responsible for overseeing the overall financial management of the business and ensuring its financial health. Their responsibilities often include developing and managing the com-pany's accounting policies and procedures, supervising the accounting team, and preparing complex financial reports for leadership.

Similar to a CFO, a controller will often play a role in financial plan-ning and strategy, including cost management and process improve-ment. They often act as the primary liaison with auditors, tax authori-ties, and banks. If you bring in a controller, they can be a helpful bridge between the accounting function and the company's strategic goals.

FOLLOWING THE DIY MODEL

If you're striving to stay lean in your spending and only bring on employees as they are needed, then it's important to build a strong accounting foundation before you consider bringing in a CFO. If you do not have a solid foundation, you will be wasting valuable time having your CFO conduct a forensic review of your accounting history and correct the errors. Instead, set your business up for success, spend wisely on building your accounting systems and processes, and then, when the time is right to bring in a CFO, set them up to help you do what they do best: grow your business!

ASSESSING YOUR BUSINESS'S
FINANCIAL AND ACCOUNTING STRUCTURE

1. **Identify Your Current Roles** – Fill out the table below to determine if your business has the right personnel in place for **accounting** and **finance** functions. If a role doesn't exist, note who currently handles it

Function	Accounting or Finance?	Do You Have This Role? (Yes/No)	Who Handles It? (Title or Name)	Is This Role Well-Defined? (Yes/No)
Bookkeeping (recording transactions)	Accounting			
Tax Compliance (filing taxes, deductions)	Accounting			
Financial Reporting (balance sheet, P&L, cash flow)	Accounting			
Budgeting & Forecasting	Finance			
Cash Flow Management	Finance			
Financial Strategy & Growth Planning	Finance			
Investor Relations/ Fundraising	Finance			

2. **Identify Gaps** – Now that you have mapped out who is handling your financial functions, it's time to look for weaknesses or vulnerabilities. Ask yourself:

1. Do you have gaps in either record-keeping (accounting) or strategic planning (finance)?
2. Are you relying too heavily on one person to manage multiple critical functions?
3. Do you have sufficient expertise at the right levels, or are there areas where you are under-resourced?

3. **Build an Action Plan** – Once you've identified gaps or risks, plan how to strengthen your financial foundation:
   1. **If you have gaps** – What immediate steps could you take to fill them? Hiring a new employee, outsourcing to a professional service, or training existing staff?
   2. **If roles are unclear** – How could you better define specific responsibilities to create clearer expectations and reduce inefficiencies?
   3. **If one person is handling too much** – Would hiring a fractional CFO, part-time accountant, or another resource improve your business and reduce risk?

By completing this exercise, you can assess whether you have a solid financial and accounting foundation or if you need to refine your current organizational structure.

CHAPTER 4

YOU'RE READY TO
LEVERAGE TECHNOLOGY

They were excited to have me and I was thrilled with the opportunity. I was hired in 2020 by a quickly growing company who thought they were ready for a CFO, though I'm not sure if they understood what a CFO could (and should) actually do. I was eager to dive into analyzing the strategy of the business and determine what operational efficiencies we could implement. Instead, I found the CEO asking me to prepare report after report, budgets, forecasts, investor reports, or whatever else he felt like he needed.

It was frustrating; most accounting programs can generate these reports at the click of a button. The issue was that while an accounting software and team were in place, the right information was not there yet. Even the most complicated reports to prepare could have been done with the knowledge of a good senior accountant or controller, which they had. Instead, they decided that they wanted a CFO. I was hopeful that I could utilize my skills and expertise to interpret the reports I was preparing. Unfortunately, that didn't happen either. The CEO seemed to want to look at the reports as sort of a "check the box" or "this is what I'm supposed to do" activity without actually leveraging the actionable insights that I was providing from the existing data in order to improve the financial health of the company.

I watched as spending far exceeded the budget, with no further investigation or consequence. I watched as the CEO approved purchases that had not been planned for. The CEO felt that his business was doing everything that businesses needed to do and that the company would never run out of funds. They created a budget; they hired a CFO; they looked at reports (and disregarded the value of most of them). This company was not ready for a CFO for three primary reasons: 1) the CEO was not ready to listen; 2) they didn't have enough work for a full-time CFO; and 3) they could have better leveraged their technology for the financial information they wanted. In this chapter we'll be focusing on how you too can make the most of technology to streamline your work and minimize your expenses.

WHAT CAN TECHNOLOGY DO FOR YOU?

Technology can be intimidating to many small businesses or startups. Nobody looks forward to learning a new program while also working around the clock to get a new business up and running. But there are several benefits to bringing in the right technology and learning how to use it early on. It is far easier to automate your business when things are simple. Waiting until you're more established will take you extra time and labor costs to transfer your data. And let's be honest: As much as we like to pretend we'll have more time later, being an entrepreneur means you are *always* working on your business. You will not be in a better position to learn technology next year or the year after. Spend the time automating processes now to create more capacity for yourself in the future.

At the same time, you don't necessarily need to leverage technology for every workflow as a new business. Choosing technology, like any other business decision, should follow the CPR methodology. Will the technology support the core of your business? Is the activity a priority? And is the technology a critical resource at a price point that you can afford?

For example, customer relationship management (CRM) systems are very popular with businesses to manage their sales. They can help a sales team efficiently plan routes to customers and improve productivity. They can automate messaging to increase sales and profitability. Generally, CRMs have a great return on investment for most businesses, including yours. However, if you're not yet selling products then there is no point in paying for a CRM just so you have them once you're ready. It's just common sense. If you're not ready to use it, you do not need to get it. There is an order in which you should bring in your technology.

One of the first things every business needs is a method to manage money and record transactions. At its most basic level, this is typically a business bank account, business credit card, and accounting program. With a little research, you can often find a low-cost solution (or even cash-back or rewards benefits) for meeting your business's financial needs. Perhaps even more importantly, though, you should seek solutions that integrate with each other. With a little extra research on the front-end, you may be able to hold off hiring a bookkeeper or accountant for quite some time as you grow.

Most accounting software on the market today is designed to integrate with major credit cards and most medium to large banks. The benefit to this is that your transactions can automatically populate in the accounting software for you to review and approve. Accounting software can often suggest the accounts that transactions should be recorded in. It's rare for most new companies to need a complex chart of accounts set up by an accounting expert. In the beginning, most company founders may be able to manage their own accounting if they select programs and companies that work together to streamline data sharing.

CORPORATE CARD CONSIDERATIONS

We don't often think of our corporate credit cards as technology, but I've included them in the conversation not only because of their potential integration with your accounting software, but also for their ability to provide you with additional benefits and features that will allow you to streamline and save. For example, many corporate credit cards have expense management programs at no additional cost. This allows you to see trends in where and how you're spending and how it compares to the money you're bringing in. If you're an established business, this is a great opportunity to determine what additional benefits and services your credit card might offer. If it doesn't offer anything, now may be the time to shop around and determine if it's worth it to make a switch.

What else can your corporate card do for you? There are credit cards that allow you to manage employee spending by setting spend limits or requiring approval on certain purchases. This allows your employees to make buying decisions while also creating fiscal guardrails around spending. It's one way to promote a culture of financial responsibility.

You can also find business credit cards that are tailored to the needs of your business. For example, some cards are designed for businesses with frequent travel. If you know you have or will have employees traveling for sales or trade shows, you may be able to find a corporate card that allows your employees to scan in their travel receipts and integrate them with your accounting and payroll software. Cards with travel rewards like hotel discounts or airline miles allow you to earn perks. These perks can then be given to employees as an enhancement to their benefits package, with no additional cost to you or your business. That is smart spending!

Most importantly, if you decide to sign up for a corporate card or already have one, make sure that you use it and pay it off monthly to avoid interest payments from overshadowing the perks!

HUMAN RESOURCES AND PAYROLL

If you have brought in your first employee or employees, it's time also to bring in human resources (HR) and payroll technology. You may also see this referred to as enterprise resource planning (ERP). These systems are essential to ensure:

1. You are consistent with your HR information (some of which needs to be stored confidentially) and payments
2. You are making the appropriate withholdings from your employees' paychecks
3. You are managing important paperwork, contracts, and company policies

Paying your employees correctly and on time is a big deal for you and a huge deal for them. Make the process easier on yourself by finding an appropriately sized and appropriately priced HR and payroll tool to use that can automate the process. Many accounting softwares offer a payroll program that you can activate for an additional fee, making one less program for you to keep track of. If you choose programs that are outside of your current accounting system, you'll want to ensure that they can integrate with your bank account and accounting software to facilitate withdrawals and transaction recording.

Some entrepreneurs anticipating fast growth and the need for more bells and whistles may be enticed to bring in a robust ERP system. I strongly recommend you not spend on an ERP until it is absolutely necessary for your business. They tend to be pricey programs and can be more complicated, using up your two most precious resources at the start of your business: your time and your money. There will hopefully come a time when investing in an ERP makes sense, but it's been my experience that most small businesses and startups can operate without them.

Instead, you'll want to find the best and simplest program to help you manage your employee onboarding, training, and payment. The system you choose should keep a digital record of your signed contracts and records of data. Many HR systems also help to generate important documents like employee manuals, vacation policies, and organizational directories for you to use internally or to share with parties who may need to contact multiple members of your organization. Again, the goal is to streamline and automate as much as possible so that you, the busy founder or CEO, are not spending valuable time rifling through piles of papers and manila folders trying to find the documents you need.

CONTRACT MANAGEMENT TOOLS

What is one tool that can potentially save a business thousands of dollars but most small businesses and startups don't have? That would be a contract management tool. In its simplest form, a contract management tool helps you keep track of all of your outstanding contracts for your business—those overhead costs you need to operate your business, such as website hosting, accounting software, cell phone plans, and security systems.

Each of these overhead expenses has a cost, contract terms, and renewal process. I have seen companies spend thousands of additional dollars on auto-renewals of contracts they don't need any longer. Regardless of whether you are a startup or a well-established business, it makes no sense to pay for services that you are not using. As a business owner, you do not need to be wasting your time sorting through emails and the pile of PDF downloads on your computer to try and find the terms of your contracts.

Without a contract management tool, it's easy to lose track of what payments you have going out the door and when, particularly for contracts that charge you annually. The good news is that you can create your own contract management tool with a simple spreadsheet in Excel or Google Sheets on your company's shared drive. You'll want to track the following:

1. The company name and contact information
2. The terms of the agreement
3. The value of the contract
4. When the next payment is due
5. When the contract renews
6. The termination clause details
7. A link to the digital contract

Every single business should have a contract management tool to track these expenses. Many companies I've worked with are surprised to uncover costs that have been flying under the radar for months or years. This simple system is another guardrail to limit unnecessary spending from happening. If you don't feel comfortable creating your own spreadsheet, there are contract management tools available on the market for a very reasonable price. However, like with most tools, the only way it works is if you use it!

INDUSTRY- OR COMPANY-SPECIFIC SYSTEMS

There are many other systems that make sense for businesses to help streamline and automate their practices. The core of your business will determine which systems initially make the most sense for you. Here are a few systems to consider based on the type of work you're performing most often.

1. **If you have heavy sales** – It is worthwhile to invest in a CRM system. These systems can range from as simple as automating your customer email sequence, to robust systems that can plot out the most efficient sales route, source new potential

customers, and create daily prompts or reminders for your sales team to check in with clients. There are out-of-the-box CRM solutions or you can have a CRM that is customized to the specific needs of your organization. It is worth evaluating the price on both. While a customized system might cost more up-front, having it perform tasks specific to your business may save you a tremendous amount of time and boost your revenue more than a one-size-fits-all solution.

2. **If you are in retail** – You'll need inventory management software to track the products you manufacture or purchase, those you sell, and those that get written off due to damage, spoilage, or theft. Tight inventory management is crucial to the successful management of retail businesses but you do not need an overly complicated or expensive system to do so. I would, however, advise against trying to go the DIY route of tracking in a spreadsheet. The amount of manual labor to update each time you make a sale and reconcile against the physical count is most likely not where you need to be putting your energy as a new retail business. Finding an affordable system that allows you to barcode and scan is worth your time back.

3. **If you are in manufacturing** – You'll need systems to manage your supply chain process. That means having systems to handle your procurement and use of raw materials. This system should integrate with your inventory management system and accounting software for a seamless flow and real-time updating of your raw material usage, product creation, and sales. Managing your scrap rates and the amount of inventory you're holding will be important financial measures for your business to track and regularly analyze for improvement.

4. **If you're in an industry that has certain professional standards** – You'll need whatever programs are required to collaborate with others in your field. For example, if you're in engineering, architecture, or construction, then a CAD program is a necessary initial investment in technology. If you're a writer, you may find programs like Scrivener or First Draft Pro to be instrumental in developing your content. If you're in healthcare, you will likely be required to use HIPAA-compliant systems for communicating health information with patients and storing patient records. Research what commonly used programs are in your specific industry and then discern if they are something you need to have or if it's a nice add-on that you can bring in at a later stage.

PLAN FOR THE FUTURE

There are an infinite number of programs, softwares, and tools that businesses can add in an effort to improve (or attempt to improve) efficiency. As your business grows, it makes sense to bring in more technology to support your operations. I have seen companies overburden themselves with complicated or expensive systems with far more functionality than they can possibly use because a talented salesperson convinced them they needed every bell and whistle on the market. This illustrates why it is important to plan your technology into the future. Don't lose sight of the CPR approach and don't spend a dollar that you don't need to spend.

Start by identifying what technology or software programs you'll need. Then identify what milestone will trigger the need for that technology. For example, you may need a tool to help you with the customer support experience where customers can submit inquiries, service tickets, or complaints. But this is not a tool you need until you have a product or service available to the market with a customer base that is buying. You may not even need this type of program right away if your sales volume is low. In that case, determine what sales volume would be the milestone to trigger the purchase of your customer support program.

Other programs to consider incorporating in your plan include marketing and sales tools, data analytics tools (if you anticipate a high volume of data in your business), productivity and project management tools, or contract signing software. When deciding what you need, also consider your level of savvy with the systems and your time and desire to learn the program. With project management, for example, there are several user-friendly programs which work for many businesses and have short video tutorials and self-learning tools to teach you how they work. Then there are complex project management programs. While I love using them and am well-versed in the technology, these are not programs that I recommend to most businesses who are new to project management software because they offer more functionality and complexity than most new businesses really need and the learning curve may be steep and frustrating.

TAKE AN INVENTORY

This exercise may help a new startup business, but it will be especially valuable to existing businesses who are looking to get smart about their spending and efficient with their management.

1. Take an inventory of all of your technology tools. What software, websites, apps, programs, spreadsheets, and systems are you currently using in your business?
2. Evaluate each program to determine if you should keep it, eliminate it, or upgrade it. Good questions to ask are:
   a. Is this program essential to running the business?
   b. What does it cost and are there opportunities to save money (e.g., renegotiating the contract, reducing the service level, etc.)?
   c. Does it integrate (and is it integrated) with our other products like bank accounts, credit cards, and accounting software?
   d. Are there other alternatives on the market that are worth researching?
   e. Can this process be simplified, automated, or integrated in some way to save us more time or make the process more efficient?

Making smart technology choices will allow you to delay bringing a CFO into your business. Remember, a CFO should not be operating as your report generator. Most accounting softwares can do that for you, or you can bring in a senior accountant or controller for more complex financial transactions. Needing financial reports is not a trigger to bring in a CFO, though. Your CFO is your strategic part-ner and right-hand support for making strategic growth decisions and taking your company to its full potential when you are ready to listen. Don't waste their talents and your money on having them printing profit and loss statements.

The goal of business technology is to take work off of your plate to better manage your business processes. With a bit of creativity and a realistic, common-sense approach, you may be pleasantly surprised to find that there are multiple ways to improve the efficiency of your business to save you time and mental energy. Then you can channel that mental energy back into what matters most in your business!

CHAPTER 5

YOU'VE CREATED A FINANCIALLY RESPONSIBLE CULTURE

Have you heard the story of the janitor at the NASA space center? The story goes that during a 1962 visit to the NASA space center, President John F. Kennedy was touring the facility and came across a janitor sweeping the floor. President Kennedy stopped his tour to introduce himself to the janitor and inquired about the work he was doing. The janitor responded, "I'm helping put a man on the moon, Mr. President."

I love this story because it illustrates an important point about company culture and the importance of aligning the team to work toward a common goal. No task is too small or too unimportant. Every single person and every single action plays a role in the mission, whether it be to release a life-changing piece of technology, serve a community the highest quality food, or put a man on the moon. Culture is a critical element of operating a successful business. A poor culture in which people feel disempowered, disengaged, or uncertain about their future may work for a few companies who churn and burn through employees. For most successful companies, a healthy culture in which people feel valued and understand their role in the big picture produces better outcomes.

In a 2023 article by the *Harvard Business Review* on why workplace culture matters, Michael McCarthy, instructor at Harvard DCE Professional & Executive Development and host of *The Happy at Work*

Podcast, stated, "Workplace culture is not just about sticking a list of values on a wall in the break room and then going about your day. It's a commitment that every person in the organization, including senior leadership, will model their behavior to support those values. The idea of letting harmful or hurtful behavior slide is not acceptable in organizations that truly embody a healthy workplace."

One of the best things a founder can do for their company is establish a healthy and financially responsible culture from the start. A financially responsible culture means that each person in the organization understands the importance of each dollar the company has, spends, and brings in. It means a shift away from viewing businesses as abstract entities that can absorb whatever cost and spending the employees feel like, and instead finding a purpose and place for each dollar that goes out the door. If you can do this effectively in your organization, you will be able to save yourself the cost of hiring a CFO earlier than necessary.

OUR RELATIONSHIP WITH MONEY

The financial culture of our company starts with us as business leaders. Regardless of business acumen, each of us has a different experience and relationship with money. There are mindsets similar to those of my immigrant grandparents, who are incredibly frugal with their spending and operate with a DIY mindset to try and take care of most things themselves. There are those with the mindset of scarcity—regardless of how much they have in their bank accounts, they make fear-based decisions based on the belief that they don't or won't have enough. There are people who feel uncomfortable with money and repel it (as soon as they get money in they immediately spend it or give it away). And there are those who seem to be money magnets, who value it and treat it with respect. They spend wisely, knowing that money enjoys movement and that more will flow back to them. What is your relationship with money?

The financial culture we create is a reflection of how we live. I used to tell my teams, "Spend the company money as if it were your own," until I realized how unhelpful that advice is. Many people, including business leaders, have poor money mindsets in their personal lives, and there I was asking them to bring that to the business. We take ourselves with us wherever we go. So, if you know you want to create a financially responsible culture in your business, it's best to start by evaluating your own relationship with money and how you address it in your personal life, then consider how you may be able to support your teams with their own wealth education.

In my personal life, I have created a culture of financial responsibility that I share with my children. I want them to understand the value of a dollar. How do you teach that to seven-year-olds? It's in the simple acts, like showing them how much toothpaste to put on their brush and explaining why we don't squirt excess globs down the sink. It's showing them how to get to the end of the ketchup bottle or why we don't overload our plates with food and then throw it away. From a very young age, my kids have understood that what we have is purchased with money that we work for. And when we save it in one place, we can spend it in other areas and on things they enjoy more, like a trip to the local ice cream shop or a family vacation.

Your financial culture is all about what behaviors you'll tolerate and what behaviors you won't. It's about what types of spending habits you encourage, what types you'll discourage, and what you'll promote or incentivize. If you're starting a new business, this is a key time for you to decide how you want to show up for yourself and others when it comes to your finances. It's not the job of a CFO to do that for you, now or in the future. If you are working with an already established business, it's time to reflect on where your business is currently and where you want to be regarding your financial culture. Changing an established culture is difficult, but it can be done if you have a clear vision and are willing to lead by example.

It starts with you! Think about what spending habits you currently have in your business. When you travel, what type of plane ticket or hotel room do you buy? When you are buying a meal with the company credit card, where are you dining? What personal expenses do you allow your business to absorb? Do you buy things without doing proper research or regret your purchases later? Do you avoid looking at finances altogether because you're too busy working on other things?

Now ask: Would you be okay if your business partner, sales leader, senior accountant, or team intern had the same approach to the company's money? If not, it's time to reflect.

The truth is that the way you spend will be passed on to your co-founder or first employee. They will pass on these spending habits to their team leaders, who will pass them down the line to their teams. Creating a financially responsible culture is not just about spending thoughtfully—it's about making financial discussions at all levels a regular part of the job. Finances become everyone's responsibility, regardless of department or role. Financial responsibility becomes part of performance reviews and how employees are rewarded. And it is so much more than simply staying within budget.

Like with the NASA janitor who put a man on the moon, your own company janitor can practice financial responsibility by simple acts like not throwing away rolls of toilet paper until they've been completely used. Yes, that is the level of granularity I mean when it comes to financial responsibility. Toilet paper costs the company money and throwing away rolls that are two-thirds used is unnecessarily wasteful and disrespectful to the money, risk, and effort that it took to bring the revenue in the door to buy that toilet paper.

This type of spending extends to every level and every position within the organization. It's not about being stingy or making life unnecessarily difficult—it's about instilling an appreciation for every dollar your organization has, valuing it, and joining together in the collective effort to utilize those dollars in the best way possible to keep the organization going and the people employed at a fair wage. Your employees are going to follow your lead when it comes to spending. If they see you having a careless attitude or spending extravagant amounts, then they will feel it's okay to do the same. I don't care how well-funded your business is; you cannot afford to take your eye off of your finances. Let's look at two examples where an irresponsible financial mindset sank what were two successful companies.

WeWork

WeWork is a company that provides coworking and office spaces for businesses and freelancers. They sought to revolutionize the office space and offer unique and more affordable office space solutions to the entrepreneurs and startups who exited the traditional workforce during the Great Recession of 2007 through 2009. With rock climbing walls and kombucha on tap, small businesses flocked to the space and WeWork expanded rapidly around the world. By 2019 the company was valued at nearly $47 billion dollars. Yet in November 2023, WeWork filed for Chapter 11 bankruptcy. What happened?

When the company revealed its public prospectus in 2019, it raised serious questions from investors about its governance and profitability, resulting in a disastrous IPO. Most fingers pointed at WeWork's CEO, Adam Neumann, who was said to use WeWork as his own personal piggy bank. The company and CEO spent money on things like a $60 million Gulfstream G650 business jet; hosting the Creator Awards, which featured celebrity judges and live performances for tens of millions; and six private properties for Neumann and his wife totaling $90 million that included a house with a private waterfall and three-story waterslide.

WeWork established a careless financial culture and disregard for corporate governance. With added pressure from external factors like the COVID-19 pandemic and the Federal Reserve raising interest rates, it ultimately collapsed under the weight of its poor financial planning.

ENRON

Named by *Fortune* magazine as "America's Most Innovative Company," Enron was a successful energy and commodities business founded by Kenneth Lay in 1985. By 2000, the company claimed $101 billion in revenue. The next year, it all came to an end in one of the largest accounting scandals of its time. Enron was found to have a financial culture that was individually, institutionally, and systematically rooted in fraud and corruption.

This culture can be traced back to the first years of the company, when Lay covered up illegal trading by two of his employees and was quoted telling them to "keep making [them] millions." Scandal after scandal continued and each time, Lay and his executive team found creative ways to wriggle out of trouble. On top of this, the company employed a cutthroat culture which inspired the documentary *The Smartest Guys in the Room*. Each year, the company would follow a "rank and yank" approach to grading their employees and firing the bottom fifteen percent. This created an ultra-competitive atmosphere that further encouraged employees to lie, deceive, and manipulate in order to meet financial targets.

While Enron had all of the so-called checks and balances in place as evidence of corporate governance, corporate governance has more to do with the mindset and attitudes of a company's leaders than with the number of boxes a company checks off on an audit list. Kenneth Lay set the foundation and those behaviors spread to the more than 20,000 employees that eventually worked for Enron before its demise.

SHIFTING MINDSETS ABOUT BUDGETS

If I were to ask you, "What is a budget?" what would you say? It might be something like, "The amount we can afford to spend in various areas of our business," or, "The target expenditure for our teams or financial statement line items." And if I were to ask you, "What is the goal of a budget?" what would you say? Most people generally answer, "To stay within budget."

If your answers are aligned with the answers I commonly hear, then you have learned budgeting as it is commonly taught. The perception of budgets, whether personal budgets or business budgets, is that they are the maximum spending limit you're allowed to have for things. People pat themselves on the back for being financially responsible when they create a budget and then pat themselves on the back again when they spend to those limits. Unfortunately, this approach often encourages and rewards people for spending the full budgeted amount as long as they don't go over.

For example, I once worked with a manufacturing company that had $20,000 left in their communications budget at the end of the year. Rather than finish the year grossly under budget, they quickly looked for ways to spend the money, hiring contractors to do unnecessary projects to fully utilize their allocated funds. Their fear was that if they came in under budget, then in the following year they would be forced to work with a new and significantly smaller spending limit. On top of that, they feared they would face consequences in the next year if they weren't able to stay within that new spending limit. The company was inadvertently incentivizing its teams to overspend due to their approach to budgeting.

Budgets should be looked at as a control or a guideline rather than a spending limit. I am an avid deep-sea diver, and I look at budgets in the same way I look at my oxygen tank meter as I explore underwater. The meter on the tank allows me to gauge the total amount of oxygen I have and estimate an approximate amount of time I may be able to spend exploring. My goal is never to push the tank to its limits and use every last breath of air available. I don't swim around aimlessly until I notice my air supply is in the danger zone and then hope I have enough to get me to the surface. If I want to have a good dive, I plan in advance. How deep do I want to go? What do I want to explore? The extent of my exploration is limited by the capacity of my oxygen tank, but I never strive to empty the tank.

Your budget is there to let your team know that there is an absolute limit as to what they're allowed to spend. There needs to be accountability when budgets are not adhered to. If your response to exceeding budget is to shrug your shoulders and say, "Better luck next year!" then it's not worth having a budget at all. There are occasions in which extenuating circumstances may cause an individual or team to exceed a budget, but those explanations should be clear, explainable, and not the norm. Your business cannot afford to run out of oxygen.

POOR BUDGETING MINDSETS

When looking at how you approach budgeting, you also have to look at your policies around budgets. Businesses with a "use it or lose it" mentality often create two problems:

1. They indirectly encourage teams to pad their budgets as much as possible
2. They incentivize needless spending at your financial year end

A more financially responsible approach to budgeting would be to explain to your teams that the budget is not a goal to hit, but a limit to avoid. Incentives should be based around how teams are able to innovate and save funds. That may mean regularly looking to renegotiate contracts, exploring the travel rewards and discounts that your credit cards or banking institution offer, or staying on top of your contract management tool and eliminating any unnecessary payments.

Another poor approach to budgeting is to set the same budget amount each year. The same-as-last-year approach creates mediocrity and is wasteful. Budgets should be created as accurately as possible based on what you know and forecast for the coming year. It is worth spending time on the front end of each budgeting cycle, going line by line with spending to develop the most accurate total possible. Instead of padding budgets with a buffer in accounts, set the expectation that certain excess costs may be allowed with specific approval. Buffers allow for excess waste instead of strategic spending.

The last poor budgeting mindset is assigning tasks to stay within budget. What I mean by this is mandating a reduction in headcount to meet budget or mandating a 2 percent reduction in cost of goods sold to meet budget. Focus on creating a financially responsible culture that reduces headcount not because the budget forces you to, but because there was excess labor that your company didn't need.

If your managers are always looking to make sure that they've hired the appropriate number of people as a part of the company's financial culture rather than hiring as much as their budget allows and then firing when the budget demands otherwise, you'll end up with a more utilized workforce and smarter spending year-round.

Establishing a financially responsible culture means that your people will naturally be looking for ways to save or spend smarter. With a poor budgeting mindset you end up cutting where things don't need to be cut because you spent on things you shouldn't have bought. You end up not buying things like that new technology that would have prevented a data breach because your sales team stayed in a pricey hotel at their last conference.

ESTABLISHING A FINANCIALLY RESPONSIBLE CULTURE

If you have an operating business and are trying to shift the culture to be more financially responsible, there are a few things you can do to help motivate your teams and change the way they think about spending and saving.

1. **Create campaigns where employees are challenged and incentivized to save money across the company** – Come up with rewards for people who identify and enact money-saving measures. Encourage teams to think creatively about ways to save or more efficient ways to work.

2. **Set up financial education programs for all employees as part of their benefits package and training** – Teach them

about personal finance, how to use a 401(k) or prepare for retirement, how to manage debt and save and invest wisely, etc. The more you can support your employees in creating their own healthy relationship with money, the more they'll bring that mindset to your business.

3. **Demonstrate that you'll no longer tolerate irresponsible financial behaviors** – If an employee is violating rules around spending, give them a warning along with an action plan to change. If they don't change, then they no longer work for your business. Treat financial irresponsibility with the same seriousness that you would treat bullying, sexual harassment, or poor ethical decision making.

The stories shared in this chapter illustrate the impact that a leader's financial mindset can have on the trajectory of their business. Creating a financially responsible company starts with you at the trunk and spreads to your employees like the branches of a tree. If you are steadfast in your care for the financial culture of the company and lead by example, your leadership team and their associates will likely follow suit.

Changing a company culture takes time and consistent, deliberate action. Having a financially responsible culture is absolutely critical to the success of your business. Don't put this as an action to take care of in the next financial year. Start now and start with you. There's never been a better time.

LAUNCH YOUR FINANCIALLY RESPONSIBLE CULTURE

If you're a new business, make sure that you create a financial culture that will be ingrained in your organization as you grow. If you're currently running a business, I have some additional work for you to shift your company culture. These are some immediate actions you can take to help quickly evolve:

1. Perform a gap analysis of where you are currently and where you need to be when it comes to budgeting and spending.
2. Schedule a town hall meeting with all of your employees and include a discussion about financial responsibility. Speak on the importance of establishing a healthy financial culture and relationship with the resources of the business.
3. Implement a financial SMART goal into every employee's performance management process. This goal should be tied to their compensation and bonus (if applicable).
4. Schedule a meeting with your leadership team to reinforce the same financial points covered in this chapter and encourage them to cascade the information down through their management chain.

If there is one chapter you work to implement in your business, I hope it is this one. The importance of establishing a financially responsible culture cannot be overstated. It becomes the foundation that will impact nearly every other aspect of your business. Do it well and the results will speak for themselves.

CHAPTER 6

YOUR LEADERSHIP TEAM KNOWS THEIR NUMBERS

Here's an easy question: If you had to work for someone, would you want to work for someone you trusted or someone you didn't trust? Of course you would want to work for someone you trust. Trust is a key factor in most successful businesses. In fact, in an article published by the *Harvard Business Review* titled "The Neuroscience of Trust,"[1] researchers found that compared with people at low-trust companies, people at high-trust companies reported:

1. 106 percent more energy at work
2. 76 percent more engagement
3. 74 percent less stress
4. 50 percent higher productivity
5. 40 percent less burnout
6. 29 percent more satisfaction with their lives
7. 13 percent fewer sick days

Those are some pretty impressive statistics! But what is it that causes employees to have trust in their leadership team? The research found several key areas that help build trust in company employees, including:

---

1 Zak, Paul J. "The Neuroscience of Trust." *Harvard Business Review*, 31 Aug. 2021, hbr. org/2017/01/the-neuroscience-of-trust.

1. Recognizing excellence
2. Inducing "challenge stress" (creating difficult but achievable jobs or goals)
3. Giving people discretion in how they do their work
4. Enabling job crafting (employees have a greater say in the projects they work on)
5. Intentionally building relationships
6. Facilitating full-person growth
7. Showing vulnerability

One additional factor that contributed to building trust was "sharing information broadly." If you want to create a financially responsible culture, it is imperative that you and your leadership team know your numbers and that you share that information with your organization regularly. You want to encourage your employees to always be looking for new ways to save or spend wisely, but you also need to show them the collective results of their efforts.

Knowing your numbers goes beyond looking at your income statement or balance sheet. There are key numbers and ratios that each department or employee should have a solid understanding of beyond their budget. In many businesses today, these numbers are referred to as KPIs, or key performance indicators. KPIs are quantifiable metrics that measure a business's performance on important objectives. They can be high-level and apply to the entire company, specific by departments, or even tracked to teams and individuals.

Unlike traditional goal-setting, when a person may say, "I want to achieve a 10 percent growth in sales this year" or "I want to increase my social media engagement by 27 percent over last year," KPI metrics should not only be measured against previous performance. KPI numbers should be compared within the company, but also measured with industry benchmarks. This is particularly important if you're a new business and don't have a "normal" to base your KPIs on. A number that might seem impressive within a startup ("Wow, our revenue went up 12 percent from last year!") may not be as impressive when compared to the industry average ("There was a boom in the industry and most companies averaged revenue growth of 15 to 20 percent").

Comparing your ability to meet your KPIs to others in your industry can make what appeared to be good KPIs look bad or what appeared to be bad KPIs look good. Your KPIs, when analyzed both within the company and against the industry, give you great context to understand your performance. If you understand what factors drive your KPIs and you share that information with your employees, you empower them to make changes and work toward better outcomes.

A LESSON FROM THE BANKING INDUSTRY

In my many years in the banking industry, I heard one particular phrase repeated so often that it feels like it's tattooed on my brain: Know your numbers; meet your numbers; no surprises. I'm grateful to have been trained in this mindset from an early professional age because it's become a key guide for each business I've started, worked for, or consulted with. I hope that it becomes your new mantra too.

Know Your Numbers

As a business leader, you must be fluent in the key metrics of your business. You need to be aware of how much you are spending on human resources, how much each employee costs, how much is your sales team spending to generate revenue, what you spend on travel to meet with clients compared to the revenue, and other expenditures that relate to the business.

Every single employee of your business costs you money in the form of their salary. That is why every single person at the company has a responsibility, either directly or indirectly, to increase revenue or decrease costs. You cannot afford to have someone at your business who is not delivering you some sort of financial value. How do you determine that value? Through relevant KPIs on things that are within their control.

To determine what your industry KPIs are, you need to look at who is aggregating the data for your industry. There may be multiple sources that can provide this data to you. For example, companies looking for operations or technology benchmarks often refer to a publication from Gartner. Search for which large consulting firms provide the relevant KPI data for your industry and then compare your performance against them.

As you bring in members of your leadership team, knowing the KPIs of the business should be a part of their onboarding process within the first 30 days. Every individual who manages a function of the organization should be aware of the metrics that are most important to that role, how they're calculated, and what the industry averages are. This early education on the importance of KPIs is in step with maintaining a strong, financially responsible culture.

Ultimately, your KPI numbers become like a GPS that lets you know the direction in which you need to steer your business to get to your desired destination. Your KPIs can provide you with insights about the cost and efficiency of onboarding new customers. KPIs can provide data about fulfillment rates for customer orders. They can also influence how you manage inventory, recruit for new positions, and invest in marketing campaigns. That is why it's imperative that every leadership team knows their numbers.

Meet Your Numbers

Most business leaders I speak with who have a budget for their business have the goal of staying within or under budget. Budgets are absolutely an important part of meeting your numbers, but they're still just a part of it. The problem with budgets is that they can be poorly designed from the start. They may follow a same-as-last-year approach to spending, which is a lazy approach. Employees may artificially pad budget numbers to give themselves more of a cushion when unexpected expenses arise. Some companies even create budgets that aren't sustainable for the business because the expenses continue to exceed revenue with no visible plan for course correction. For example, I once advised a CEO who was paying a generous salary (equal to his own) to an investor who believed that because he had equity, he was entitled to compensation. This expense alone had a successful company at the verge of bankruptcy.

If you are not meeting your budget numbers, it's important to set aside the time to figure out why as soon as possible. Ideally, you'll approach proactively meeting your numbers and holding monthly financial check-ins with your leaders. If expenses or revenue are deviating from what you expected, you need to address it as quickly as possible. Financial missteps are like embers of a fire. If you're not keeping your eyes on them and putting them out as quickly as possible, they can turn into huge fires, causing more damage and taking more time than anyone has to spend.

Establishing KPIs is another tool that can help you meet your numbers, but only if your employees are being held accountable to those KPIs. For example, if your sales team's KPIs reveal that the cost per new customer acquisition is too high, rather than allowing them to operate in the same manner until they're out of budget, you need to reassess their sales approach. Once the team meets their customer acquisition KPI, they will be better equipped to stay within or below budget for the year. While not all KPIs are financial, a lot of them often walk hand in hand with budgets when it comes to meeting numbers.

No Surprises

This is perhaps the most important piece of knowing your numbers. "No surprises" means you're not waiting until the end of your fiscal year to evaluate how you performed financially. Financial reporting and financial variances should be analyzed monthly within any business. Waiting twelve months is too long and may make it too late for you to take any form of corrective action.

Instead, I recommend that leaders analyze their numbers weekly. Teams should come together for financial analysis monthly. Organizations should come together for a financial check-in quarterly. Not only is this a part of transparency—it's a key feature of establishing and maintaining a financially responsible culture. When your culture is financially responsible, then all decisions at an organization are made through a financial lens. Employees know that they will have to explain why they chose to allocate resources to one area instead of another. Leaders will not be surprising their teams with emergency layoffs at year-end to salvage the budget or letting employees know that they will not get a raise or bonus the following year because the company can't afford it.

Regular evaluation of spending also means that in instances where one-off, outlier-type expenditures or events arise, the company can identify them and course correct in other areas if needed. Things happen with every business, whether it's a regulatory change that requires a product to be reworked, a raw materials shortage related to a country's political climate, or a natural disaster that impacts your ability to work. Surprises are a part of life. "No surprises" means taking control where you can to minimize the unexpected. The best way to do this is for your leadership team to know their numbers.

One of the best ways to assure that this process works successfully and assure that your leadership cares about their numbers is what I coin the Empowerment to Accountability (E2A) Principle. First, you need to make sure that in addition to your leadership team knowing their numbers, you empower them to do the necessary work to achieve them. Secondly, you make them accountable for meeting their numbers and avoid surprises.

In order to institutionalize the latter each functional leader should have clear and *smart* goals tied to their business area and their individual performance. Doing so ensures that: 1) you have clearly defined these goals (numbers); 2) you have agreed on a clear methodology to calculate, track, and report them; 3) they know what impacts their numbers; and 4) they are proactively managing and making decisions that are aligned with the health of their numbers.

A final word of caution here: You as their manager should be coherent and consistent when it comes to the performance review, their appraisal, and any impact that it may have on their future role and compensation. One of the most frustrating experiences during my time at the bank was when a manager in a performance review told me that I had done great but that I still was not getting a raise and my bonus was actually being reduced from the prior year. I asked him what I could have done differently and he responded, "Nothing, keep doing what you are doing, you are doing great." His message was completely disconnected from the company's actions as it related to my compensation. After having to take in this absurd situation and digesting the frustration, I tried to take proactive action to ensure that would not happen again. So, during our next meeting, when we set and agreed on my goals for the following year, I asked very specifically what goals he had for me as leader of our team and what and how he was going to measure them. I wanted to avoid being disappointed again, but more importantly I wanted to work hard to achieve my newly assigned goals.

A year later, after requesting periodic feedback and being made to feel that I was knocking it out of the park, there came another good-but-not-good-enough performance rating, and with it another disappointing compensation outcome for me. When I asked for feedback on each of the goals (company, department, personal), my manager confirmed that indeed, I had excelled at meeting all goals that we had set out for me during the year and that my performance was outstanding. However, other people "perceived" that I could do more (yet he was unable to tell me what) and because of that, here I was, once again paying the consequences of a lousy performance management process.

My advice: Set out clear goals, make sure that your team knows what they need to do (and if applicable, how they need to do it), define a clear and objective evaluation criteria, have meaningful feedback sessions, and reward (or hold accountable) your team accordingly.

WHY YOU DON'T NEED A CFO

When companies begin to take greater control of their finances, their spending, and their KPIs, there is often the desire to bring in a CFO to play a role in the evaluation. The challenge that arises is that oftentimes CEOs will offload the financial responsibility onto the CFO, removing knowing their numbers from their list of responsibilities. The reality is that every CEO needs to know their numbers, regardless of whether they have a CFO or not.

If you find yourself wanting to bring in a CFO so that you can avoid learning or dealing with the finances of your business, you are making a critical error. Instead, become fluent in your finances. That way, when the time is right to bring in a CFO, you can have meaningful conversations about the performance and strategy of the company rather than being advised what to do without understanding the "why."

Learning key financial ratios and how to interpret them does take some time and effort. However, they're not difficult to do. With the help of your accounting software, you should be able to calculate your ratios and know your numbers at any time. Doing so will make you a more effective leader and save you money by not hiring a full-time CFO.

Don't be afraid of finances. It's an education you can't afford to miss.

TRACKING WHAT MATTERS
AND SETTING REAL TARGETS

It's time to roll up your sleeves. Gather your leadership team. If you're a team of one right now, that's perfectly fine too. The goal of this exercise is to build a simple but powerful system to track the numbers that truly matter for the health and growth of your business.

Step 1 – Identify Critical Metrics by Area

Think about the core areas of your business: sales, marketing, operations, finance, and customer service. For each one, ask yourself: "What number would tell me, at a glance, if this area is healthy?"

Examples:

1. **Sales** – Number of new leads per month, conversion rate from lead to sale
2. **Marketing** – Cost per lead, website traffic growth rate
3. **Operations** – Order fulfillment time, error rates in delivery or production
4. **Finance** – Cash balance, gross margin percentage, monthly burn rate
5. **Customer Service** – Customer satisfaction score (CSAT), number of support tickets resolved within 24 hours

List two to three metrics per area that would give you real visibility into performance.

Step 2 – Set Specific Targets

Once you know what to track, it's time to set targets: clear numbers that define success. Think: What would a good month look like? What would a warning sign look like?

Examples:

1. Increase monthly website traffic by 15 percent over the next quarter
2. Maintain a customer satisfaction score of over 90 percent
3. Keep gross margin above 65 percent
4. Reduce fulfillment errors to less than 1 percent of all orders
5. Targets give you a line in the sand: Are you ahead, on track, or falling behind?

Next to each metric, write down a clear, measurable target for the next 90 days.

Step 3 – Challenge Cross-Functional Thinking

Business areas don't operate in silos—they influence each other. Push yourself (and your team) to think about how one area's performance affects another.

Examples:

1. If marketing drives a surge in leads, how will sales and operations handle the volume?
2. If fulfillment errors rise, how will that impact customer satisfaction scores and repeat sales?
3. If customer service response times slow down, what effect might that have on referrals or churn rates?
4. Draw a simple cause-and-effect map connecting your key metrics across departments

CHAPTER 7

YOU MAKE DATA-DRIVEN DECISIONS

Over the past few chapters, I've been focused on helping you build the most effective and efficient team possible for your business. This chapter is no exception! It's pretty obvious in business that we should be making decisions based on the best intel or data that we have available to us. Every so often, I've worked with a CEO or business leader who makes a decision that is not data-based and unfortunately I've seen it come back to bite them. The CEO approving it does not mean the decision was a good one or one the business could support. Analyzing your data will help ensure that the actions you take make sense.

But what about that gut instinct makes some leaders so good at what they do? Making data-driven decisions does not mean ignoring your gut instinct. Instead, data helps you determine your best viable options to choose from rather than taking an unsubstantiated route. If you have data at your fingertips, it's simply unwise *not* to use it. And if your data doesn't support your decision-making, then you have an invitation to explore why you feel so strongly about that decision in the first place.

There are nine key ratios that I am going to share with you here. These ratios are foundational for every business, regardless of your size, industry, or years of experience. Ratios help you to determine what is going on below the surface. What are the drivers of revenue and how do your expenses compare? There are many more ratios that are specific to what you do or what business stage you're in and I encourage you to continue your education on learning the key ratios that will be most important in supporting your decision making. Remember that ratios and data are an important piece of your leadership team knowing their numbers and developing a financially responsible culture.

If, because of your history with money and finances, these last three chapters have left you feeling nervous, I encourage you to continue to lean in and learn more. Discomfort with money or discussing finances is common in Western culture, but it is just a cultural mindset and one we can push through. In Eastern countries, like Japan, the discussion of money, wealth, and personal finance is commonplace. Acknowledge your own feelings around money. If it brings up fear or shame, it's worth your time to explore where those feelings come from. Then, dive in and do the financial work, like figuring out your financial ratios. It is absolutely a valuable use of your time and energy.

WHAT CAN RATIOS DO FOR YOU?

I'll get to how we calculate our key financial ratios in a moment, but first let's talk about why we need them in the first place and what they can do for us. The data itself is just that: data. It is our job as leaders to interpret that data and what it may mean for our business. For example, let's say your accounts receivable (AR) is growing month after month. One explanation could be that your sales have also increased and there is a direct correlation. Another possible reason, though, is that you are not collecting on your receivables as effectively. You may have one or a few particularly large clients with outstanding balances who are impacting the total AR. Or perhaps, in your rapid growth, your accountant no longer has time to follow up with clients for payment.

In this situation there are several potential drivers for our increase in AR, each of them requiring a different action. If your increase in AR is due to more clients not paying on time, it is a great time to determine what late payment penalties you have in place. How do you incentivize your customers to pay on time in the future? You can also look at what actions you need to take as a result. If customers aren't paying in a timely manner and you decide to implement a late fee structure for balances over 30 or 60 days, then you need to be prepared to communicate the new policy to your customers. This may include phone calls from your sales or accounting team to make an attempt on collection of the outstanding balance and then inform of the new fee structure.

Regardless of the direction you would choose, it is important to realize that this issue in your business most likely would not have come to your attention in a timely manner had you not been actively engaged with your financial ratios and trends. When you take control of your finances and are open to increasing your financial savvy, then you can further delay the need to bring a CFO into your business. Even better, once you do bring in a CFO, they should not be presenting you with any major financial surprises because you have already been on top of your company's numbers. This is the best possible track to start your relationship when a CFO joins your team!

NINE ESSENTIAL RATIOS FOR YOUR BUSINESS

Imagine sitting down at your desk, pulling up a simple dashboard, and instantly knowing whether your business is on track—or if trouble is brewing just beneath the surface. Every number you see tells a story: how much cash you really have, how efficiently you're converting sales, or whether your growth is sustainable.

In this section, I won't just define the key financial ratios you need to understand—I'll walk you through how to calculate them, what they reveal about the health of your business, and how to spot both opportunities and early warning signs. You'll learn not only what these numbers are, but how to read them like a seasoned entrepreneur steering the ship with confidence.

Revenue Growth

Revenue growth is one of the top KPIs that you should be aware of as a CEO. It measures your increase or decrease in revenue from the prior period to the next. This is something that you can and should track on a monthly basis, on a quarterly basis, and on an annual basis. It is a metric that most often your accounting software may already be tracking and reporting for you, but if not, the calculation is simple:

(Current period revenue – previous period revenue) / Previous period revenue = % increase or decrease in revenue

Your revenue growth percentage will give you multiple insights into your sales. Perhaps your revenue has grown because you've just launched a new product or a new marketing campaign. Perhaps it has slowed because of a seasonality in the industry or the loss of your top salesperson. When you calculate your revenue growth ratio, your next step should be to explain why it moved the way it did. This will help you encounter and solve potential problems while they are still small or signal to you the need to scale up your business to meet future anticipated revenue.

Gross Profit Margin

Gross profit margin ratio shows how effectively your business is producing and selling its products or services relative to the cost of goods sold (COGS). It is calculated by:

(Revenue – COGS) / Revenue = Gross profit margin percentage

A higher gross profit margin often reflects efficient production or a strong pricing strategy. Business owners can use this ratio to determine whether there is enough revenue left after COGS to cover operating expenses and invest in future growth. The higher your gross profit margin percentage is, the better position your business is in to grow.

Net Profit Margin

Your net profit margin is how much of the money you bring in you still have left after expenses are paid. This is a ratio that you need to compare both internally for monthly or quarterly fluctuations and against the industry average. Net profit margin is calculated by:

Net income / Revenue = Net profit margin

Net profit margin is an indicator of your long-term sustainability and financial health. When you compare yourself to your industry, your net profit margin might reveal cost savings opportunities or a need to optimize your processes and procedures. Compared against yourself, this vital ratio will help you identify how good you are with your spending. If revenue decreases, but you still keep spending at the same rate for months or years, your net profit margin is going to take a serious hit. Conversely, if you launch a financially responsible culture shift in your company and you see your net profit margin increase, then you know the process has been effective and you can seek ways to reward your team for their efforts.

ROI

Return on investment (ROI) evaluates the efficiency of financial investments you make, such as marketing, equipment, or expanding into new ventures. This ratio helps you to evaluate the efficiency, profitability, and strategic value of a particular investment relative to its cost. ROI is calculated by:

$$(\text{Revenue gained from investment} - \text{Amount invested}) / \text{Amount invested} = \text{ROI}$$

Knowing your ROI (or projected ROI) on projects can help you as a business owner to prioritize your allocation of resources to the areas where you get the greatest return. ROI could be calculated by product or service line to determine your most and least profitable offerings. It might help you compare the effectiveness of marketing campaigns or investments in technology like a CRM. As a brand-new startup, this ratio may not be relevant to you, but it's good to know as it will become relevant at some point.

Run Rate or Burn Rate

These ratios indicate how quickly a company is spending cash relative to revenue (burn rate) or projected revenue based on current performance (run rate). While there is a technical difference in the definition between the two, you'll find that the terms are often used interchangeably. This ratio helps business owners understand how long their cash reserves will last or how sustainable their current growth pace is. To calculate your run rate/burn rate:

$$\text{Total capital / Monthly operating expenses} = \text{\# of months before you run out of capital}$$

This ratio is particularly important for startups. Say you have $1,000,000 in the bank to put toward your new venture and you spend $100,000 per month without generating revenue. You have ten months to operate without revenue. By the end of the tenth month (and hopefully far before then), you are generating revenue, you've raised more capital, or you've decreased your expenses. Otherwise, you're out of money and business!

Customer Acquisition Cost (CAC)

Customer acquisition cost shows how much it costs to acquire a new customer, factoring in marketing and sales costs. It can help you assess the efficiency of your marketing strategies and whether your spending is justified by the revenue generated from each customer. CAC is calculated by:

$$\text{(Sales + Marketing cost) / Total customers acquired in a period} = \text{CAC}$$

This ratio becomes particularly important when you find yourself with a sales team and more expenses, like traveling to trade shows. It may also help you determine if customers are no longer as attracted to your product as they were, indicating that the product might need to be enhanced.

While this ratio isn't often helpful in the startup phase of business, it is absolutely essential once you have a base of clients. This ratio (along with the next one) can help you determine if you're bringing in enough customers and the right customers for your business. In the earlier stages of a business, this ratio may be much higher as you give away or offer enticing discounts to customers to get started. Once you've established more of a reputation and are getting referrals or positive reviews, you have more flexibility to charge for services that were once free or to increase your costs.

Customer Lifetime Value (CLV)

Customer lifetime value is the total revenue your business expects to earn from a single customer over their entire relationship. Comparing CLV to CAC can help determine if acquiring and retaining customers is financially worthwhile. It may also identify opportunities to improve customer loyalty and profitability. It is calculated by:

Average value of sale per customer x Average number of sales per customer x Average length of time a customer buys from you = CLV

Let's use Netflix as an example. Let's assume that they charge a customer $10 for a month of service, and customers pay for a full twelve months, and they retain their clients for about five years. That's $10 x 12 months x 5 years = $600 CLV.

I like to take this ratio one step further and subtract out the CAC from the CLV for a more accurate reflection of what each customer brings to the business in revenue. Once you see how much it costs to bring a customer in and how much revenue they can potentially bring to your business, you can make better decisions around customer loyalty programs and retention plans.

Employee Turnover

This ratio calculates the rate at which employees leave your company, either voluntarily or involuntarily. While this ratio may not be as relevant to certain types of businesses, others, like call centers, need to place a heavy emphasis on calculating and analyzing this ratio. Employee turnover is calculated as:

Number of employees who left during a period / Average number of employees = Employee turnover

A higher turnover may indicate underlying issues like poor job satisfaction, inadequate compensation, or mismanagement, which can lead to higher hiring and training costs and lower productivity. If you have a high ratio, it's time to look at what additional benefits you may be able to offer to your employees and how those benefits affect your other ratios. There are ways to offer non-direct-cost benefits by offering things like a flexible work schedule, remote working options, or additional PTO days.

This is a key ratio for any business with a human resources department. The cost of hiring and onboarding new employees is high. Employee turnover is an area that affects many areas of your business, both directly and indirectly. Therefore, it's important to stay on top of this ratio as a gauge for the health of your company culture.

Cash Flow

Cash flow measures the inflow and outflow of cash in a business. A positive cash flow indicates healthy liquidity, ensuring that a business can meet its obligations, invest in opportunities, and handle unexpected expenses. A negative cash flow may signal financial strain and identify a need for better cash management. Cash flow is calculated as:

$$\text{Total cash in} - \text{Total cash out} = \text{Net cash flow}$$

Cash flow is critical to making financing decisions. Your cash flow determines if you can pay for things outright or if you need to use credit. It also helps you prioritize paying your accounts payables and managing your accounts receivables. You need cash to operate your business, which is why this is an important ratio for every business to track.

TAKING RATIOS A STEP FURTHER

There are so many more ratios and KPIs that are worthwhile to use for your specific business. Ratios are an important part of financial management because they are often the first step in identifying issues or problem areas and initiating important conversations. Not every ratio or KPI your business has will be financial in nature, but they will all have an influence on your company's finances.

Employee engagement is one example. If your employees are not happy, that may reflect in how they treat customers, which affects your sales and customer retention rate. Having a tool (like a quarterly survey) to measure your employees' level of engagement would benefit you in identifying and remedying the non-financial problem before it becomes a big financial problem. Without understanding employee engagement and working to fix it, the result will likely evolve into employees quitting, which will be detected in your employee turnover ratio. Rather than wait until you see it impact your employee turnover ratio, you can be proactive and create a KPI around employee engagement.

Once you understand how your numbers work together and what types of activities or actions drive your ratios and financial performance, you'll be able to make better, data-driven decisions. For each of the ratios that I've listed, there could be an entire subset of potential drivers that impact those ratios. Spend the time to understand what your drivers are and what KPI you need to have to keep these nine ratios in line. Every company will be different in the ratios it needs, but there is one common truth for every business: You need to understand your data to make informed decisions.

EXERCISE

CALCULATE YOUR KEY RATIOS

First, a word of caution. We live in a world that is saturated with excess data. Unfortunately, so much data can lead to the famous "analysis paralysis." It is critical that as you start looking at data from your company and industry you structure it in a way in which it will be transformed from just data to actionable insights. By doing this, you will be able to make more accurate and faster decisions.

I encourage you to take time today to figure out at least a few of these ratios (or others more suitable to your specific industry) for your own business, just to see how non-scary or complicated it is. You may even learn that your accounting software calculates some of these for you!

Then create a plan of when you would like to calculate and analyze all of the ratios each month for your business. Set a date and stick to it. I always recommend doing this at the beginning of every month. Once you feel comfortable in calculating and analyzing the above ratios, challenge yourself to dive further into possible drivers of those ratios. These are more opportunities to seek relevant ratio calculations or establish KPIs tied to your employees' performance. The more you're willing to understand your numbers, the better your business will be for it, and the longer you may be able to hold off on hiring a CFO!

CHAPTER 8

YOU ARE WILLING TO OUTSOURCE

What are your feelings about outsourcing? Over the years, I've found that some people resist hiring outside of their companies. Perhaps it's because it feels outside of your control. Perhaps you view it as more costly on an hourly or project basis (which it usually is) and you assume it makes more sense to handle things in-house. Or maybe it's because many business owners have a strong DIY drive and try to take on as much as possible.

Outsourcing, however, can be an incredibly cost-effective way to bring in the experts you need at the scale you need them. How do you know, though, when it makes sense to outsource versus having someone in-house? There are a few gauges I use to help make this determination. (Keep in mind that these are suggestions and what makes the most sense for your business may vary.)

IDENTIFY CRITICAL ROLES

Critical roles are those positions that are a non-negotiable need for your business. They are positions that drive you to getting to your first customer and dollar of revenue. For example, a tech company that specializes in software must have a software developer as part of its management team. A bookkeeper, however, could be outsourced, as the decision to have one in-house or not would not impact your path to revenue. Critical roles must be aligned to the CPR methodology at the priorities and resources levels.

Assess If You Have Enough Work

A common trap I find new businesses falling into is hiring when they don't have enough work. This is problematic in a few ways—not only are you paying for access to services that you can't fully utilize, but you are creating a poor work environment for your employees. While overutilization can quickly lead to burnout, underutilization impacts morale. Underutilized employees end up feeling disengaged and unmotivated. It can also lead to frustration and feeling undervalued. If you don't have enough work for an employee to be fully utilized, the position should probably be outsourced.

Determine If the Need Is Temporary or Permanent

Setting up a new business may require the knowledge of experts. There are times when we need the advice of those who specialize in a technical field, whether it's legal support with setting up your entity structure and preparing contracts, tax support to ensure you are registered appropriately, or accounting advice to set up a proper chart of accounts. However, that doesn't mean we need their advice or knowledge on an ongoing basis. If the need is temporary, this is a sign that you should outsource the work.

FUNCTIONAL OVER PERFECT

I have great respect for individuals who want to do things perfectly from the start. The better off you are with your accounting setup, legal documentation, and HR process, the fewer issues you may encounter in the future. The reality of launching a business, however, is that we often don't have the financial resources (or the time) to aim for perfection. Instead, the goal is to be functional.

This means looking at what you and your team need to do to get things moving and bring revenue through the door. Once you've identified the key roles and milestones for the first stage, you will have a clearer idea of what you can outsource for the time being. Keep in mind that just because you outsource a service now does not mean you need to outsource it forever. It makes me think of the quote from business leader and author Marshall Goldsmith, who said, "What got you here won't get you there."

Businesses are ever-evolving organisms that require new skills and resources at each stage of growth. At the beginning, when you may be relying heavily on using capital provided by investors, it is critical that you operate as lean as possible. When you reach the stage at which you are relying less on investor money because you're generating revenue, you can shift to hiring more people in-house. In other words, when your core has a heartbeat, you can start thinking about starting to train that body and taking it to the gym.

OTHER BENEFITS OF OUTSOURCING

There are many underlying costs to hiring besides the salary or hourly wage itself. Plus, there are legal rules and regulations you need to follow as an employer related to safety, company policies and procedures, employer benefits, taxes, withholdings, and more. As an employer, you take on a very real legal liability and may find yourself in trouble if you're not familiar with the rules.

I once had a friend who found himself incurring unnecessary unemployment costs after firing an employee for multiple violations.

Although the employee had repeatedly missed deadlines, violated company policies, and received verbal warnings, my friend had no written documentation to support the termination.

There were no written warnings, no incident reports, no performance improvement plans (PIPs), and no formal records of counseling meetings. Without a paper trail such as signed warning notices, email confirmations summarizing discussions, or manager notes outlining the issues and corrective expectations, he was unable to prove that the termination was justified when the employee filed for unemployment benefits. As a result, the company's unemployment insurance costs increased unnecessarily.

Hiring employees means having an HR function as part of your business—another role that you need to hire, outsource, or DIY. It means having an employee handbook and onboarding procedures. It means taking responsibility for maintaining morale and providing benefits. If you need to have work done for your business but it's not related to your MVP, it is worth looking into outsourcing the position at the start. If you don't have experience in hiring and managing employees and they are not a necessity for your business, it is worth looking into outsourcing. Doing so may save you from unnecessary and expensive complications.

POSITIONS YOU SHOULD OUTSOURCE AS A STARTUP OR SMALL BUSINESS

There are many positions that make sense to outsource as a startup or small business. In fact, you may be outsourcing some of them already. Let's start with accounting. If you're using accounting software, like QuickBooks, you may want to outsource a bookkeeper to help ensure your chart of accounts is properly set up and customized for your business needs. A bookkeeper can help a marketing agency create separate income categories for different service lines (like social media management, advertising, and consulting), or assist a product-based business in tracking inventory, cost of goods sold, and shipping expenses correctly, which can save time and prevent mistakes down the road. I would also recommend outsourcing your taxes to a CPA to ensure they're filed accurately and on time. Eventually, you may hire an in-house tax accountant, but many businesses find it beneficial to leverage the shared knowledge and experience of a tax firm rather than rely on one individual for all of their tax preparation.

Payroll and human resources are other departments I often recommend new businesses consider outsourcing. There are a wide range of payroll processing companies that can help manage key aspects of payroll administration. These services typically handle calculating gross and net pay, withholding and remitting payroll taxes, issuing payments to employees through direct deposit or checks, and filing required tax forms such as W-2s and 1099s at year-end. Some providers also offer additional services like onboarding paperwork, benefits administration, and compliance monitoring, depending on the complexity of your needs and the size of your business.

Marketing is an area in which you may consider outsourcing as well. Marketing is a necessity for nearly all businesses, regardless of size. However, the role of marketing may not be a full-time position depending on the type of business you are and the type of marketing outreach you're looking to do. For example, if you expect to reach most of your customers through social media platforms, you may consider outsourcing to a social media and SEO specialist who can be hired to create and schedule marketing campaigns. You may also outsource your web design and maintenance services if they are not within your wheelhouse.

Once you start hiring employees and need onboarding and tech stack setup processes in place, it may make sense to hire an IT management company. These companies typically work on a per-employee/per-month fee basis while taking the process of getting each of your employees set up with their needed technology off your plate. They will create your specified tech stack (laptop, monitor, or whatever other tech products your employees require) and preconfigure each product with the necessary software and onboarding support. When you outsource to an IT management firm, their fulfillment process is triggered each time you hire a new employee. They may take on the responsibility of monitoring and managing devices, and handle the return of products when employees leave their position.

How do you know when it's time to make the transition from outsourcing a role to hiring in-house? It's simple! When the cost of outsourcing exceeds the cost of employing a person to do the work, it may be time to make the switch.

EXERCISE
CPR THROUGH A CRITICAL LENS

Now that you have a clear view of your current team and responsibilities, it's time to re-evaluate your resource roster from Chapter 2 through a more strategic lens: criticality and core value.

Step 1 – Identify Core vs. Outsourceable Roles

Make a chart with two columns: In-House vs. Outsource.

Then, consult your resource roster. Highlight the roles that are critical to the core operation, culture, and daily decision-making of your business. These are roles you should likely keep in-house (e.g., leadership, strategic).

Flag roles that are specialized, transactional, or support-oriented but not central to your unique business identity. These are strong candidates for outsourcing (e.g., bookkeeping, payroll processing, tax preparation, IT support).

Transition to Step 2 – The role categorization in Step 1 is crucial because it clarifies which functions are essential to your business's identity and which can be delegated to external providers without compromising your core operations. By identifying outsourceable roles, you've pinpointed areas where external expertise or efficiency can enhance performance, freeing up time and resources for strategic priorities. Step 2 builds on this by requiring you to define specific outcomes for each outsourced role, ensuring that your outsourcing decisions align with your business goals and deliver measurable value.

Step 2 – Define the Outcome You Expect from Outsourcing

Before jumping into researching outsourcing options, be clear on what you want to achieve by doing so:

1. Reduce costs
2. Improve service quality
3. Increase flexibility or scalability
4. Access specialized expertise

Write a short statement for each role you're considering outsourcing: "I want to outsource [function] to [achieve desired outcome]."

Step 3 – Research and Referrals with a Purpose

Begin researching providers for these outsourceable roles, but focus your search based on your goals, not just their cost.

1. Look for firms or freelancers with proven experience in your industry or business size
2. Seek referrals from peers, advisors, or trusted networks
3. Compare service levels. What's included? How responsive are they? Can they scale with you?
4. Ask for case studies or client references if possible
5. Create a shortlist of two to three vetted providers for each function you're considering outsourcing

CHAPTER 9

YOU ARE LEVERAGING
YOUR NETWORK

One lesson I've learned in business is that great things can happen over a cup of coffee (I don't just say that because I'm a coffeeholic!). I have had so many powerful, impactful, and insightful conversations in coffee shops and restaurants with people who happily shared their knowledge for the cost of a simple beverage. Over my years in the corporate world, I made it a point to connect daily over coffee with colleagues, mentors, or friends. When I started my consulting firm to help entrepreneurs and small business owners with finance and operations, I built relationships through lunch or coffee meetings. My final role as a full-time CFO came from a family member's introduction to someone who, after a coffee chat, connected me with my future employer.

As you read through this chapter, I want you to enter with the mindset that the things we do don't have to be complicated or scary. Getting the help you need can sometimes be as simple as asking, "Hey, can I buy you a cup of coffee and hear your thoughts on ___?" So, go ahead and start treating people to coffee, and as a remarkable and inspiring MBA professor taught me during a coaching session while I was navigating a career transition, "Never leave a networking meeting without asking if there is anything that you can do for the other person." That's just classy!

Launching or running a business with a financially responsible mind-set often means getting creative in our approach to problem-solving. I find myself in this same creative position once again as I start my new digital health business. Now, I've learned a lot of things and have a lot of experience over the years that helped me set up this new venture, but I still don't know everything. What I've found when entering a new field of business is that sometimes the most dangerous thing is that we don't know what we don't know.

How do we overcome knowledge gaps and get the expert help we need when we're currently operating on a lean budget that has us brewing our own coffee at home and flying economy to conferences? If outsourcing to experts is not within reach, then it's time to tap into one of the most valuable resources you may have: your network.

Shortly after launching my current company, in the spring of 2024, I was going through my mental Rolodex (remember those?) of people I knew and trusted who might be able to help me in my new business, I remembered that my cousin, Jose, is probably the sharpest technologist I know and also a person I trust completely. I made a quick phone call and discovered that he was more than happy to review our new company's plan for developing technology, the UX/UI design, and the development proposal provided by a company we were considering outsourcing to. My cousin was instrumental in raising red flags on things we needed to consider, like network security. He suggested we inquire more about the different costs that may be incurred to transition the technology from this company to our own internal management down the road. This is an area where some companies end up paying additional fees down the road, and he didn't want us to be caught off guard in the future. We are grateful for Jose's knowledge.

Then, my co-founder remembered a college friend of ours who had become a pharmacist. We've kept in touch and remained very close friends over the years, so it was very natural to reach out to her to see if she was open to being a sounding board for our new venture. Like most people who we ask for support, she was absolutely willing to share her knowledge and perspective on any of our questions or ideas related to managing medication. In fact, she wants us to succeed because the work we're doing may eventually help serve her patients and their families, making the healthcare process easier to navigate for everyone involved.

Your first business instinct may be that you need to go out and hire someone for all of the work you need and have not outsourced, but what if you tried sourcing your network first? The worst they can say is "no."

MAKING THE ASK

Did reading the word "no" just now cause you to recoil a bit? It does scare many people. It's rare when I find someone who is truly unbothered by rejection. Even still, when you do hear "no", particularly when you are asking for advice for your business, the consequences of that answer are usually minimal. You should not take their answer personally; take a moment to professionally thank them, and move on to see who else you know or can hire! Being an entrepreneur often means being a bit tenacious, a bit scrappy, and able to put aside your fears for the sake of helping your business grow.

More often than not, people generally want to help and are willing to do so. People within your network will often give you a more favorable rate or sometimes not charge at all for their knowledge and/or skills because they believe in your project and want you to succeed. In some cases, the people that help you early on may benefit from a permanent job offer when you can afford it. It's absolutely worth making the ask to people who may help you and your business avoid incurring a cost.

LEVERAGING YOUR NETWORK

I have three steps that I recommend taking when it comes to leveraging your network to help save you money and keep you operating with a CPR mindset. It's not rocket science. In fact, to you the steps may feel quite obvious. Sadly, some new or established businesses don't think of using their network as a tool for growth. Many businesses don't take full advantage of the breadth of their network, instead just tapping into a few close resources. To operate with a CPR mindset, you'll need to be more intentional and strategic about how you engage your network—and that's exactly what these three simple, high-impact steps will help you do.

Step 1 - Fully Identify Your Network

The first step to leveraging your network is identifying who is a part of it. I really encourage you to stretch your mind to figure out who you know and how they could support your business to get you to your first client or your next stage of growth. I start with close friends and family, since I've found they are often most willing to be supportive. Then I look to the next layer out. These may be friends or acquaintances that I'm not as close with, but have still maintained some sort of connection.

I also look to networking groups and places where I hold active memberships. These connections are more often to result in free consultation and reduced rates for services. My stretch connections are those people who I may not have been in contact with for a while, but may still be willing to help, like former professors and university alumni, former employers who I maintained a positive relationship with, friends of friends, or people I've connected with at conferences and events.

Step 2 – Establish Clear Expectations

The next step is to be transparent and honest about your request. Be clear about what you are doing and what you're hoping they can help with. Let them know if this is a one-time request or if you're looking for their ongoing support. Share if you are able to compensate them in any way or if you are asking for a favor. Set the expectations for what you're looking for so that they can decide if they want to opt in or not.

I have been on both the side of asking for support from others and of being asked to support others. A few years into working as a full-time paid consultant, a friend of mine asked if I'd be willing to consult for his business. I shared that I was happy to help and provided advice on ways he could get the best possible start to his new endeavor. Based on how often he consulted with me for business decisions, it felt like we had developed a working partnership that may have eventually evolved into a paid position. Some time later he stopped asking for help and was off and running with his new company. I was left a bit surprised and frustrated in trying to understand what my role had been and why it suddenly changed without much discussion.

While people may assume that my friend was taking advantage of my free advice, he was only leveraging his network. I had agreed to be of service and was happy to help. However, the lack of clarity around expectations on both sides of our relationship created a challenging end to what was a great collaboration. We're still friends, but that experience taught me the importance of being absolutely clear on: 1) what you're willing to give; and 2) what you're hoping for from the other person, whether that is compensation or a future position.

Step 3 – Establish Your Advisory Board

If you thought that boards were just for large, publicly traded companies or non-profits, it's time to shift your mindset. Even a small startup can benefit from having what's known as an advisory board. The purpose of boards may vary slightly from organization to organization. However, most boards have two things in common: 1) they have different skill sets than you; and 2) they offer a multidisciplinary approach to running your business.

Advisory boards are different from a board of directors in that they're not representing shareholders' interests and they don't have a say in who is running the company. Instead, your advisory board becomes your close network of trusted advisors. They tend to be proactive in guiding you through strategic decision-making because they have a vested interest in the success of your business. Your advisory board may work pro bono or provide coaching for an hourly rate.

In my new business of tech-enabled healthcare, we have an advisory board composed of a primary care physician, a pediatrician, a pharmacist, a psychologist, and a technologist. They are not full-time hires, but consultants that provide input to validate what we're doing and that we're in sync with what they need. Our relationship is a two-way street: we get the expertise that we need at an affordable price and they become an ambassador for our company. We pay our advisory board hourly, only when we use their services. I have found that having a knowledgeable advisory board is an easier and more cost-effective way to get the knowledge you need without hiring on employees.

The one thing your advisory board should not be doing is advising on the day-to-day operations of your business. This is an important line that should not be crossed. If your advisory board is too entrenched in the day-to-day, they may begin to take on a role more similar to an employee or co-executive and can no longer offer that valuable outsider perspective to you. That's not to say that an advisory board member couldn't eventually become a part of your team, but while they're serving on the board, this boundary must be in place.

FINAL THOUGHTS

There are a few last important points before you start picking up the phone or firing up your email to reach out to your network. First, make sure you can very clearly explain the mission and vision of your business to your contact. Get comfortable explaining to them that you are currently operating with limited resources. If you're not operating with limited resources because you just raised $10 million from investors, then don't make the unrealistic ask of them to work for free.

If this chapter has you feeling concerned because your network is limited, then seek out ways you can build your network. Look for local business organizations, industry support groups (especially if you're in tech or healthcare), entrepreneurial organizations that support your cause, alumni groups, etc. It is never too late to start building your network. If you don't have a network yet, then let today be the day that changes.

Lastly, leveraging your network can allow you to hold off on hiring a CFO because you may be able to tap into that financial knowledge through your own network or advisory board. Throughout my career I have consulted and advised numerous businesses. It's part of being in the ecosystem of entrepreneurship—we support each other when and how we can. If you're a startup, you won't need a lot of advice from a CFO or someone with a similar background, but they could help provide valuable knowledge about your business structure or raising capital. Eventually, as you need more support, you can look at bringing in that CFO (or a different CFO) on a fractional basis.

BUILD YOUR IDEAL ADVISORY BOARD

An advisory board can become one of the most powerful tools in growing and strengthening your business if you approach it intentionally. Use this exercise to design and begin building yours.

Step 1 – Envision Your Ideal Board

Take a moment to imagine that anything is possible. If you could handpick an advisory board with no limitations, what types of expertise and perspectives would you want around your table? Think beyond titles; think about knowledge, experience, and connections.

Prompt Questions:

1. Do you need legal guidance, financial expertise, or HR experience?
2. Would you benefit from someone deeply connected to your target customer base?
3. Would having a distribution partner, vendor, or retail contact be strategic?
4. Is there an industry veteran whose experience could help you avoid common pitfalls?

Make a list of five to seven ideal profiles or skill sets you'd like represented on your advisory board.

Step 2 – Map Your Network

Now, look outward. Start with the vision you created and then comb your network intentionally to find people who fit those profiles.

Ask yourself:

1. Who in your current network matches one of the skill sets you need?
2. Who do your close contacts know that you could be introduced to?
3. Where are the clear gaps and which networks, associations, or events could help you fill them?

Next to each ideal profile, write down one or two names you know or places to search to find the right person.

Step 3 – Make the Ask (Clearly and Confidently)

Once you have your shortlist, it's time to reach out. Be direct and professional. Explain who you are, why you're building an advisory board, and what kind of advice or involvement you are seeking.

Proposed Structure for Outreach:

1. Introduce yourself and your business clearly
2. Explain the advisory board's purpose (e.g., strategic input, occasional guidance, no legal fiduciary responsibility)
3. Share why you believe they would be a strong fit
4. Specify the level of time commitment you are asking for (e.g., quarterly meetings, occasional emails)
5. End with a polite ask, and stay gracious if they decline
6. Draft a simple outreach email or LinkedIn message template you can customize for each person

Remember that a "no" is not a dead end; it's an opportunity to ask if they know someone else who might be a great fit. Often, the advice or connection you need is just a coffee meeting or a single brave ask away. I recently proved this by taking the courage to comment on a LinkedIn post of an ideal advisor for my new company. He graciously accepted my request to connect and tell him more about what we are doing, and a couple of meetings later we are proud to have him as an advisor!

CHAPTER 10

YOU'VE HIRED A FRACTIONAL CFO

By now you have hopefully realized that this book is not about how to avoid CFOs like they're the plague—it's about how to bring them in at the right time and in the right way to witness the greatest benefit to your business. Because I am a CFO, some people may be confused why I would not suggest hiring someone like me full-time from the start. However, my primary role as CFO is to serve as your right-hand guide to make sure you're making the smartest and most financially sound decisions that will allow your business to grow. Encouraging you to hire a full-time CFO before your business is truly ready for one would be poor advice and run counter to my purpose.

The previous chapters highlighted many of the reasons why you are either not ready for a CFO or how you can delay incurring the cost of a CFO. At some point, my hope for you and your business is that you *will* reach the point where a CFO is the next right step for you to take. This may be for any of the following reasons:

1. Your current financial and accounting employees are exceeding their workload capacity or have reached knowledge limitations
2. You have additional compliance needs that cannot be addressed by your current team
3. Your business has reached the point where it's scaling and you need a multi-departmental approach to growth

4. You may not be quite ready for Series A financing, but
    you're getting close to that point

If you're currently experiencing any of these in your business and it's not something you can quickly fix by outsourcing or leveraging your network, then it may be time for you to bring in the help of a CFO.

CFOs add value to your business by helping you see opportunities that you may not have seen for yourself. They are strategic advisors—not just numbers people—who can help you connect the dots between teams and departments, as well as money out and money in, to make sure goals are aligned and inefficiencies are rooted out. Best of all, you can employ the services of a CFO without incurring the salary of a full-time CFO. This role is known as a fractional CFO!

WHY HIRE A FRACTIONAL CFO?

Fractional CFOs are a growing business's answer to having access to CFO knowledge without the price tag that usually comes with it. Most companies in an early growth stage don't have enough work for a CFO to do full-time. Remember when I discussed in the CPR resources about only bringing in a person when you have enough work for them? Well, fractional positions are like the asterisks to that statement. If you don't have enough full-time work for some positions, you may be able to create a fractional position to fit the amount of work you do have. Don't spend a dollar that you don't need to spend!

Initially, your fractional CFO may feel like they have a lot of work to do. It can take some time to get well-versed in the financial history of the company while gaining an understanding of how each of the departments operate. The benefit to fractional CFOs is that the number of hours they commit to your business each week may ebb and flow. In my experience, once I've got a good understanding of the business and can get some financial systems established, the business can run almost on autopilot until the next time it needs to level up.

A CFO is an expensive position to bring into your business. If the time has come to hire one, it's important that you set your CFO up for success so that they can hit the ground running. That may mean hiring on or outsourcing work to an accountant or CPA who can do a forensic audit of your accounting and financial statements to ensure everything is in order. There may be historical transactions that need reclassifying. Your books should match your bank statements and your investment documents.

EXPECTATIONS FOR YOUR FRACTIONAL CFO

Your fractional CFO will have a lot to do in their first 100 days on the job. Regardless of how clean your financials are, it is necessary for your fractional CFO to do their own look backward and make sure your accounting and records are in shape. They may find additional gaps that need to be closed. During this review, your fractional CFO may find areas of opportunity for you as the business leader to take a look at. It may be areas where company employees are spending too much time or resources and not getting a good return. They may find AR or AP issues that your accounting team has fallen behind on managing due to fast growth or poor habits. Their overall review of procedures during this exploratory stage will set the groundwork for determining what comes next.

Once your fractional CFO has determined that your processes are in order, including having proper month-end, quarter-end, and year-end closes, they can move on to the next step. They will need to evaluate your reporting landscape and determine the appropriateness and any potential gaps in internal and external reporting. This may mean evaluating the company's current investor and board reports and actively serving as the liaison between the company and the board of directors.

From there, your fractional CFO will need to spend time exploring and evaluating compliance with industry and governmental regulations. Are you meeting the requirements in each geographic area in which your company operates? Are you collecting and remitting taxes properly? These are issues that plague companies of all sizes. I have witnessed smaller companies not remit tax statements because they didn't have any income and face penalties for failing to report that they had zero income. I have also worked with medium and large companies that did an excellent job of handling the compliance requirements for their parent companies but didn't realize that the compliance of their subsidiaries had fallen by the wayside. A fresh set of eyes from a fractional CFO will give you a new holistic view of your company and areas for improvement.

Once your company is in a solid financial state and following all necessary compliance requirements, your CFO is ready to look ahead into the future to help you, the business owner or leader, make sense of your company data and use it to drive informed decisions. Like the saying, "If you want different results, you have to do things differently" advises, your fractional CFO will help you and your leadership team to think outside of the box and avoid the trap of complacency. But they can only help you if you help them.

SETTING UP YOUR
FRACTIONAL CFO FOR SUCCESS

If you've done everything mentioned in the previous nine chapters and you still feel like your business has a financial knowledge gap, your business might be ready for a fractional CFO. Keep in mind that the fractional CFO you bring in may or may not become your full-time CFO later on, which is why it's important to set them up for success. You will want someone who can support you in the short-term and also stay with you into the future (or set you up in a good position).

What does it mean to set your CFO up for success? In my experience, one of the most important things is to be open and transparent about your accounting, your finances, and how you run your business. Your CFO is not there to audit you and judge you; they're there to discover the truth of your financial position and help guide you in the right direction. Sometimes business owners or CEOs feel shame over past financial decisions, poor spending choices, or questionable judgmental calls and they try to hide that information from their new CFO. Let me be clear: Numbers don't lie, and employees talk. If you don't tell me something, your financials will, either through what you've recorded or what you've avoided recording that raises a red flag.

I have a vivid memory of being brought in as a fractional CFO for a company that wasn't necessarily making the best financial choices. As any CFO would, I began my process by digging through their accounting transactions to get a picture of their processes, spending, and system of recording. At one point I came across a rather large transaction; several thousand dollars had been spent to rent out a luxury box at a sporting event. The CEO made no mention of the expenditure and there was little documentation explaining why the company had spent on a lavish expense when they had yet to bring much of a profit through the door.

It wasn't until the week before the event that the CEO approached me to inform me of this purchase that he claimed was a reward for a few employees. How or why they had earned this reward had not been determined. In fact, the company's performance at that point was definitely not reward-worthy. Still, the CEO hoped that he would be able to sneak this expense by me and not have to be held accountable for it. But the books told all.

Your best bet is to lay your cards on the table and understand that your CFO is there as your ally and partner, not your mother-in-law or your crabby boss. Treat them as a strategic partner and communicate accordingly. If you're forthright about what your past and current issues are, then your CFO can move into action and get you back on track. You may have done things wrong in the past, but that does not mean that you need to continue to do so going forward. If you lie or hide things, you're wasting their time and your money.

YOUR FRACTIONAL CFO
JOB DESCRIPTION AND KEY DELIVERABLES

It's time to bring in your fractional CFO. In order to do that you need to develop a job description and list of key responsibilities and deliverables for the position. What is it that you most hope your CFO will help you accomplish? What other tasks would you like them to explore? As the business owner, you can tailor the responsibilities of the CFO to the specific needs of your organization. If you are clear on what you need, then you'll be able to more easily determine who the right person is to get you there.

Complete the steps below to create a clear job description and list of key deliverables:

1. List Your Top Three Financial Goals: What are the most important outcomes you want your CFO to help you achieve?
2. Identify Five to Seven Key Responsibilities: What tasks, areas of oversight, or strategic initiatives should your CFO own?
3. Note Additional Projects or Explorations: Are there special projects (e.g., fundraising, system upgrades, forecasting) you want them to tackle?
4. Tailor the Role to Your Business Needs: Think about where your business is today and what kind of support will help it grow faster and smarter
5. Write a Draft Job Description: Using your answers, outline a short job description that you can refine and use when recruiting the right candidate

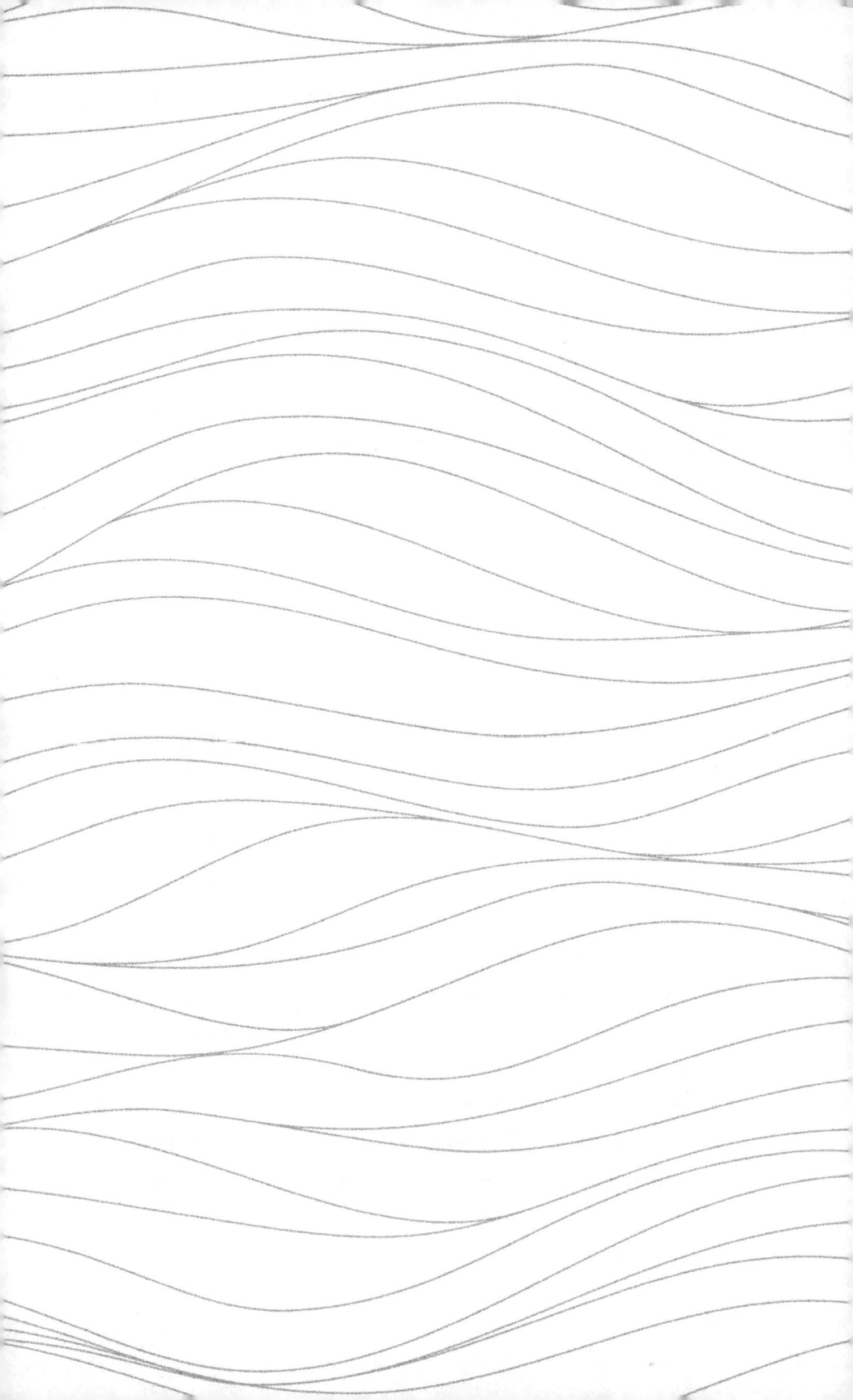

WHAT'S NEXT?

Congratulations on reading the ten reasons why you don't need a CFO! If you've been able to implement one or several of these strategies in your business, then you should have a better sense of if and when it's the right time to hire a CFO. I highly recommend starting with a fractional CFO as they're a great way to test the waters and make sure that a CFO is right for you. Once you see the value in their work and you know you're ready to listen to their advice, you may be ready for the next step.

You've done the hard work. Starting a business from nothing or carrying on a generational business and keeping it relevant is no small feat. You should be really proud of that! It's also exhausting work, which makes it completely understandable when some businesses fall into a state of complacency or "this is how we do things." We all need a break from the madness of being a startup. Falling into routine may feel good for a while. But if you recognize that you've been existing in your comfort zone to the tune of complete stagnation, then the next section of this book is for you.

Many businesses initially grow in an organic way, taking on challenges and opportunities as they come along. It can be a great way to start, but often cannot take you to the next level. It reminds me of the phrase, "If you want different results, you have to do things differently." Your CFO may be the catalyst you need to increase your margins, make more money, expand your locations, reach more investors, or whatever else you would like to try. Your CFO will usher in an era of real, strategic growth. When you're ready for it, read on!

▼

PART II

FIVE SIGNS THAT YOU DO NEED A CFO

CHAPTER 11

YOU ARE READY TO LISTEN

If you've made it this far in the book, chances are you are in a state where you're ready to or have already implemented the recommendations in the first section of the book. Whether your business has reached the point where you need a full-time CFO or you're being proactive about preparing for your future, I'm really glad you're here. I want to see more businesses flourishing and exceeding financial performance at levels they never imagined they could reach.

Achieving these new levels of success often means that we need new ideas, fresh input, and outside support from people who have gone through what we're preparing for. When you are open to new ways of doing things, even when you've had success in your old ways, you have overcome one of the biggest hurdles in hiring a CFO. You have put your ego aside. You understand that your business is its own unique organism that needs more than just your know-how to thrive.

Let's reflect back on Chapter 1 and the reason why I mentioned that some business owners are not ready for a CFO: They're not ready to listen. In my experience, there are three common reasons why business leaders would not be ready to listen to a CFO:

1. Your business is not at the right developmental stage to listen to a CFO
2. You don't have time to listen
3. Your ego gets in the way

As company leaders or managers, it's important that we are regularly assessing and reflecting on our own states of being, our mindset, and our maturity. Taking the self-assessment mentioned in Chapter 1 is an easy way to check in and become aware of our strengths, areas of improvement, and our blind spots. If you can be honest with yourself and you are still finding that your ego drives much of your decision-making, that is okay. That is how you are choosing to lead. With that choice comes the consequence that you will never experience the full advantage of having a CFO for your business.

There are other mentalities that may prevent you from taking full advantage of the services your CFO can offer. One, for example, is applying the DIY mentality to business. A DIY mentality is often advantageous if you're a startup or small business. Leaders who use the CPR methodology and are conscious of every dollar that goes out the door get into the routine of doing things themselves or handling projects with the expertise of their current team. This mindset is an excellent one to have . . . to a point.

The hope is that your business grows to the point where the DIY mindset doesn't cut it anymore and you, as a business leader, don't have the capacity or the savvy to take on everything. The good news is that most businesses that reach this point have more financial resources in the bank and can afford to start investing in outside consultation or can afford to expand the team with new expertise. By the time you reach this phase, you may have already tested the waters with a fractional CFO to see what they can offer your business. Hopefully you have also cultivated a leadership mentality that includes humility and the willingness to bring in strategic partners for growth.

ENTERING A STRATEGIC GROWTH PHASE

Contemplating the need for a CFO often signals that your business is entering a strategic growth phase, a point where financial bottlenecks are emerging and additional investment is needed to meet expanding customer demands. Your demand may be at or exceeding the supply of what you can produce or service. You may be entering new markets and have increased compliance needs. Bringing in a CFO is like bringing in a coach or a guide to help you reach your next financial milestones. Their role covers several areas, including making sure your company's finances are being handled correctly. A great CFO will serve as a dot-to-dot connector between your departments, identifying areas for operational efficiency and verifying that departmental KPIs or goals are aligned with the overall goals of the business.

Your CFO is also someone who speaks the language when it comes to working with savvy investors and your board of directors. While your business may have initially launched thanks to modest investments from friends and family, your next phase of pitching to investors or venture capitalists will be for larger sums of capital (anywhere from hundreds of thousands to millions). Seeking this level of funding requires a knowledgeable leader from your business to speak to things like the company's cash flow, revenue projections, operating costs, and return on investment. Remember those ratios I covered in Chapter 7? It's one thing to be able to calculate them. It's another to understand and explain the complex interplay of how the numbers relate to each other and what is driving them. For that job, your CFO has got you covered!

Have you accomplished the core goals of your business and have outgrown what you can do alone? Congratulations! This is a great sign that you're ready for a CFO—if you're willing to listen. Strategic growth may be challenging at first because it forces businesses to operate in new ways that they may have not considered before, but if you're open to taking your CFO's advice, you'll be on an accelerated path forward.

LEAVING YOUR COMFORT ZONE

Does your company use the term "business as usual"? If so, it may mean that you have established routines and procedures for how you operate. You and your employees know what it is you need to focus on to continue generating revenue and serving your customers. For business owners who have grown a company from nothing, business as usual may feel like a welcome plateau. It's a place for you to catch your breath, step back and view the business holistically, and maybe even squeeze in some much-needed sleep!

Operating in our zone of "business as usual" can present challenges, too. I have seen this particularly in family businesses who have their way of doing things and keep operating in the same manner for decades, save for a few upgrades to technology or the way they advertise. What may have created success early on rarely lasts forever. It's like the old adage, "You rest, you rust." While that phrase is often applied to aging and exercise, it's the same with business. If you're getting too comfortable and find yourself feeling too settled, you may need someone to help you stretch your thinking.

Sound great? Having a CFO to show you new possibilities may be exactly what you are ready for, but your team may not be as warm to the idea. If you have a long-established leadership team, perhaps with a technology officer that you've had since Day 1 or an HR manager who helped take you from a few employees to multiple locations of many employees, you may find that they are reluctant to bring in someone new, especially to a role that will question them as part of the quest to improve operational efficiency.

A CFO (especially a really good CFO) will find ways to challenge the status quo. As humans, we're hardwired to be resistant to change and the unknown. Often people would rather stay in less-than-optimal situations that they know versus trying new ways of working. It is important that you understand where your team is and if they are willing to listen if you bring a CFO in. This may require a few listening sessions with your team to understand their concerns and desires for the business. Pay close attention to what you're hearing. Someone demonstrating a strong resistance to a CFO may be a red flag. As I've mentioned before, the numbers don't lie. Bringing in a CFO to comb through the financials will allow you as the business leader to see what your teams have been willing or unwilling to show you. If you have an associate, business leader, or team engaging in unethical or illegal practices, your CFO may discover it.

READY TO LISTEN

Like a coach training an athlete, a CFO training you may be the next right step for you if you are open to listening and using new advice. It's a way to reach the next level of success and compete against businesses who are bigger or own a greater percentage of the market.

To confirm that you are ready to bring in a CFO, I recommend completing these three steps:

1. Check yourself and take a new personal assessment to see if you're in the right state to listen to advice and receive honest feedback.
2. Determine what the next phase of your business looks like and what you'll need to get there. This might include needs that a CFO can support you in fulfilling, such as financial strategy and planning, cash flow management, and investor relations and fundraising.
3. Prepare for you and your team to stretch outside of your comfort zone for a strategic wake-up call that can show you new ways of operating for the next level of success.

If you have done all three, then you are ready to grow your business. Remember that your CFO is your partner in your business. They will challenge you to be better. Like a coach with a rising star athlete, a CFO's goal is to help you succeed.

MOMENT OF PAUSE

It's time to revisit the self-assessment for CEOs and founders that I discussed in the first chapter. When you feel that the time has come to bring in a CFO (or any other critical member of your leadership team), retake the personality test and reassess yourself as a leader.

You may be wondering why you should expect a different result this time. The answer, at least from my personal experience, is that as founders, entrepreneurs, and C-level executives, we live in dog years. Our roles shift constantly. One day we're building products, the next we're pitching investors, leading teams, or reinventing strategy altogether. With every pivot, challenge, and lesson learned, certain aspects of who we are evolve rapidly. It's natural for parts of your self-assessment to change as you grow. At the same time, some traits may remain consistent, and that's not a flaw; it simply highlights your dominant characteristics, the ones you can either lean into or manage more intentionally as you continue to lead and adapt.

Ask yourself the following questions:
1. How did you fare over the challenging journey of starting a company? How did it affect you as a business leader? How did it affect you personally?
2. Where are you now as a leader?
3. What support do you need to grow?

Once you've evaluated yourself, it's time to evaluate your company. Consider the following questions for contemplation:
1. How would you rate the current health of your business?

2. What are the most acute or critical areas you feel need to be addressed?
3. If you hired a fractional CFO already, what were the biggest findings that they delivered? Anything you were surprised about?

Taking these moments of pause to step back and evaluate yourself as a leader and your business as a whole is vital for healthy growth.

CHAPTER 12

YOUR COMPLIANCE
NEEDS HAVE INCREASED

It was a bit of a nightmare, really. There I was, consulting with a company on their financials, and realizing that they had kept all of their focus on their parent company. The financial health and recordkeeping of the parent company was great—they had no major issues and appeared to comply with all regulations. They mentioned that they had a few subsidiaries that operated out of different geographies and that I could take a look at those as well if I had the time.

They spoke about the subsidiaries as if they were something optional or less important, so I was clued in right away that this exploration might not be as smooth as it was with the parent company. I was right. While the parent company was focused, well-documented, and had processes in place for finance, accounting, and compliance requirements, the subsidiaries were like forgotten pieces, floundering along as best they could. They had missed reporting deadlines, organizational paperwork, and many more local requirements that differed from the parent company due to the laws of where each was headquartered.

The company had grown quickly, spinning off subsidiaries to handle new projects and different areas of operations. In the process of rapid scaling, the company leadership focused too hard on their core business and left themselves vulnerable with their poorly managed subsidiaries. My work resulted in the business incurring fines for late reporting and a few financial restatements, something that most companies never want to go through. Nevertheless, they were necessary steps to get the business back on the right path to support future accelerated growth. They weren't wrong to bring in a CFO. In fact, it was a necessary position for their company. Where they erred was in their timing.

TIMING IT RIGHT

Knowing when to bring in a CFO can be challenging. On one hand, it's often an expensive executive position that you want to make sure you can afford and that you'll be able to fully utilize. On the other hand, if you wait too long you may end up like the company above and find yourself using your CFO like a financial clean-up crew for poor practices that have gone on too long. How do you know when the timing is right?

There are three key signals that can let you know that a CFO should be added to your team:
1. You have increased compliance needs
2. You are preparing for your next round of financing
3. You have increased investor needs

COMPLIANCE NEEDS

In my own experience, one of the most complicated parts of running a business is staying on top of compliance requirements. Laws and regulations are constantly changing and it's on the business owner to stay apprised of these requirements. For example, on January 1, 2024, in the United States, the Financial Crimes Enforcement Network (FinCEN) launched a new requirement for all companies to file a Beneficial Ownership Information (BOI) report. This report was created as part of the Corporate Transparency Act to identify individuals who directly and indirectly have an interest in businesses. The penalties for not reporting are steep, running $500 per day for late filing, up to $10,000 in fines, and the potential for two years in jail. It's not something that businesses want to forget!

Yet in the day-to-day grind of running a business, these details can get lost in the shuffle. The BOI report is just one example of the many requirements businesses may have. These requirements become increasingly complex depending on where you're selling your products or services, the number of states or countries you're operating in, and the relative risk of your industry. Financial services and healthcare, for example, face far more scrutiny and regulatory requirements than a clothing manufacturer or a professional service provider.

You should aim to bring on a fractional or full-time CFO before you anticipate an increased need for filing or reporting. Bring them in before you open your second location or subsidiary in a different geography. Bring them in before you enter a new product or service industry that is different from your core business. If you do not have someone on your team who knows how to navigate compliance, tax, or industry-specific requirements, it is time for you to utilize a CFO.

NEXT ROUND OF FINANCING

If you are preparing to scale, then you may also be looking for additional investment to help finance the growth. Preparing to request and receive additional investment capital is both an administrative task and a financial task, and unless you're already quite savvy about financing, a CFO is the person you will want to guide you through the process.

Seasoned investors will do their due diligence. They will have many more questions and expect more financial disclosure than was needed in your first round of raising investment capital. You may also need to prepare a comprehensive data room covering extensive information about your company, alongside non-disclosure agreements so that the information shared with potentially interested parties does not become public knowledge.

A CFO can help prepare financial projections, business valuations, and expected returns. A CFO can also be instrumental in showcasing your business's growth potential, competitive edge, and marketing opportunities. This information helps instill confidence in investors and may result in a more successful round of fundraising.

INCREASED INVESTOR NEEDS

Once you have more investors in your business, it becomes crucial to have a dedicated point person to manage the relationships. A CFO will not only manage the relationship between investors and the company's executive leadership—they should also serve as a liaison with the board of directors. Having this point of contact allows for a unified and consistent messaging for the company and helps to manage any concerns that may arise as a result of market issues, regulatory changes, or business challenges.

Administratively, your investors will want regular communications on the state of the company. Your CFO should provide investor reviews and progress reports to keep all parties informed on the present and future state of the company. Depending on your investors and board of directors, these reports may be monthly, quarterly, and/or annually, and you should work to keep them informed and engaged with the business's performance.

As the company's CEO or leader, you may have had to handle investor relationships, board relationships, or compliance requirements up until this point. You may be pretty savvy in these areas by now. However, it is likely that you do not have the available time to take on these responsibilities anymore. Hiring a CFO to handle them is a wise move as it allows the CFO to do what they excel at and it allows you the fresh capacity to drive the strategies of the business forward.

YOUR COMPLIANCE CHECKLIST

If your business is preparing to seek a new round of investment capital, it is important that you create a task list or checklist for your CFO with your needs for the above categories. Don't assume that your CFO will automatically understand what your expectations are, particularly since companies utilize CFOs in so many different ways. It is also helpful if you can prioritize the importance of the activities you need them to complete. Perhaps tax compliance is high on your list. For someone else, ensuring that all investor paperwork is filed properly may be top of mind.

If you're relatively new to compliance and are not sure what exactly your CFO needs to do, then mark it as an important topic of conversation to have with them sooner rather than later. They can figure out what your compliance requirements are, but you will help them arrive at that discovery sooner if you identify it as an area for improvement.

1 - Increased Compliance Needs
Regulatory Filings & Corporate Governance
- Review the company's current legal structure and corporate bylaws
- Ensure all required tax filings (federal, state, and local) are up to date
- Confirm that all business licenses and permits are current
- Assess compliance with employment laws and benefits regulations

Financial & Accounting Compliance

- Review current accounting policies and ensure GAAP or IFRS compliance
- Verify internal controls and identify areas for improvement
- Assess readiness for financial audits and ensure books are audit-ready
- Confirm compliance with any industry-specific regulations

Risk Management & Insurance

- Review and update business insurance policies (D&O, liability, cyber, etc.)
- Identify and mitigate financial risks (currency, credit, operational risks)
- Ensure proper record-keeping and documentation for all financial decisions

2 - Preparing for the Next Round of Financing

Financial Health Assessment

- Review and validate the current financial statements
- Analyze cash runway and project financial needs for the next twelve to twenty-four months
- Evaluate burn rate and implement strategies for financial efficiency

Fundraising Preparation

- Review and update the financial model for investor presentations
- Prepare a cap table review and confirm equity structure
- Identify and document key metrics that investors will scrutinize

- Ensure all previous investment rounds are properly recorded and documented

Investor Readiness & Due Diligence
- Organize and maintain a virtual data room with financial records, contracts, and compliance documents
- Ensure tax filings, P&L statements, and balance sheets are ready for due diligence
- Align with the CEO on messaging and storytelling for investor pitches

3 - Increased Investor Needs & Requests
Investor Relations & Reporting
- Establish a cadence for investor updates (monthly, quarterly, or as required)
- Prepare templates for investor reports, financial updates, and key metrics
- Define a process for responding to investor inquiries

Board & Shareholder Management
- Schedule and prepare materials for upcoming board meetings
- Align financial reporting with board expectations and requirements
- Ensure board consents, meeting minutes, and resolutions are properly documented

Strategic Financial Communication
- Work with the CEO to refine investor messaging and financial storytelling

- Identify potential new investors and maintain investor pipeline tracking
- Ensure a clear road map for capital allocation and company growth strategy

Next Steps

- CEO and CFO to review this checklist within the first thirty to sixty days
- CFO to provide feedback on any additional gaps or needs
- Establish a reporting structure with your CFO for ongoing updates

CHAPTER 13

YOU ARE PREPARING TO SCALE

This is an exciting time! You're ready to scale your business to the next level. Before you hit the accelerator, though, you need to be prepared for the growth ahead. A CFO may be an invaluable guide to you to ensure that you have the best processes and procedures in place to scale effectively.

If running a business is akin to training for a 5k race, then scaling is like preparing for a triathlon. Yes, it still includes running, but there are new disciplines added and many more considerations to reach your goal. Triathletes need to have the skills and endurance for open water swimming and bike riding long distances. They have to be more aware of how they fuel their bodies and how they stay hydrated. Their tools change. The sneakers that may have been perfectly sufficient for 3.1 miles might be the worst possible choice for a triathlon. Even the mentality around running for 30 minutes is far different than the mentality needed to get through a triathlon course.

We should view scaling a business in this same way. Scaling is so much more than just hiring on extra people to take on more customers. Your processes likely need to change to account for new volume. Your software systems and equipment may not have the capability to handle the new amount of transactions or data that you're working with. And that bespoke customer service that you've become known for as a small, family-owned business may need to evolve to accommodate your new customer base. For many business owners, the struggle in scaling is doing it in a way that is within the financial means of the company, while maintaining a seamless experience for your customers.

To start, it's important to validate that you have the following:

1. A solid organization with proper documentation, solid accounting fundamentals, and a relatively smooth operating process

2. A solid onboarding process for your clients to buy from your business and a customer retention program to maintain the relationship

3. A solid onboarding process for employees that allows you to efficiently hire and get employees up to speed in a relatively short amount of time

4. Enough funds in the bank to accelerate your growth, hire additional employees as needed, and make additional investments in the technology, machinery, or other items required as you scale

Scaling is really about project management. Successful scaling happens when you have a well-thought-out plan, both operationally and financially. If you are planning to scale your business, then strong project management experience should be on your CFO's resume and be stated clearly in their job description. The CFO's role should be to handle the scaling activities, thus allowing the CEO or founder and senior management teams to stay focused on managing and leading day-to-day operations.

CFO SCALING RESPONSIBILITIES

Your CFO can help with scaling your business in many different ways, including:

1. **Financial forecasting** – Determining funding needs and growth feasibility
2. **Budgeting** – Allocation of resources across the company to support growth
3. **Investment analysis** – Evaluating growth and scaling initiatives to determine their ROI
4. **Capital-raising strategies** – Determining if loans, venture capital, or equity investments are the best way to drive growth
5. **Cost management** – Monitoring expense trends to identify inefficiencies and free up additional capital
6. **Risk management** – Identifying potential scaling issues including market fluctuations and cash flow challenges
7. **Investor relationships** – Communicating with potential and existing investors and keeping them informed of updates in the growth strategy of the business

Some people are shocked when I tell them that scaling their business should be the responsibility of their CFO, not the business owner. The CFO is in the best position to manage this process. If you have brought in your CFO early enough and they've had time to get established well before your plan to scale, then they will have had the proper time to ensure your accounting and financial processes are established and running almost as if on autopilot. This allows your CFO to have additional capacity to allocate their time to managing scaling.

Beyond managing numbers, an experienced CFO understands the full business ecosystem and can anticipate financial challenges before they arise. They can connect the dots between different business functions such as sales, marketing, and operations, ensuring that all departments are operationally and financially aligned for growth. Their analytical expertise enables them to guide strategic decision-making and ensure that the business scales profitably and sustainably.

UNDERSTANDING THE RISK MATRIX

In my own experience running a digital healthcare company, I've seen how critical proper risk planning can be. Some of the devices my team and I relied on were manufactured in China, and while the supply chain had been stable for years, we knew from our risk matrix that geopolitical shifts (including the possibility of tariffs) were a real threat to our margins. When new tariffs were suddenly imposed, increasing the cost of importing key components, it didn't catch us off guard.

Because we had already identified this risk, we had contingency plans ready: We quickly shifted part of our sourcing to alternative suppliers and renegotiated contracts to absorb some of the added costs. As a result, we were able to protect our margins and maintain financial stability during a critical growth period. The experience reinforced for us that a good risk matrix doesn't just predict potential problems, it gives you the time and clarity to respond before they become real threats.

If you are planning to scale your business, then it will be incredibly helpful for you to create a tool known as a risk matrix. A risk matrix is an important project management tool that helps businesses identify their most immediate threats and strategize ways to manage those risks. A risk matrix is a grid with one axis representing a low, medium, or high assessment of a risk happening, and the other axis representing the severity of the impact as minor, major, or critical.

A risk matrix typically includes:

1. **Likelihood Axis** – Categorizing risk as low, medium, or high in terms of probability
2. **Impact Axis** – Evaluating the severity of consequences as minor, major, or critical
3. **Color Coding** – Visual representation of risks, often ranging from green (low risk) to red (high risk), to facilitate decision-making

It's a valuable tool as it provides a visual, color-coded description of risk categories and potential risk priorities. Specifically related to scaling, a risk matrix can help you identify new potential risks from expansion, mitigate risks associated with asset allocation, and support you in making informed decisions about how to scale. Once you've created a risk matrix for your scaling process, it's important that you stay on top of it constantly. It's a tool to help you and your leadership team be proactive in taking action before potential risks surface and materialize, and if they do become issues, to act quickly to resolve them.

A CFO can leverage the risk matrix to:

1. **Identify Expansion Risks** – Assess financial, operational, and market risks associated with scaling
2. **Mitigate Asset Allocation Risks** – Ensure the company does not overextend financially while investing in growth

3. **Support Informed Decision-Making** – Provide executives with data-driven insights to optimize growth strategies

Your CFO should not only create and monitor the risk matrix but also ensure that contingency plans are in place for potential financial challenges. These may include things like cash flow contingencies to develop reserve strategies to prevent liquidity issues during scaling. It may also include debt vs. equity analysis to evaluate the financial impact of different funding sources. Another risk area is operational adjustments to make data-driven recommendations to optimize cost structures as the company expands. By integrating risk management into scaling strategies, a CFO provides the stability and foresight needed to scale efficiently while protecting the business's financial health.

Scaling is not just about growth—it's about *sustainable* growth. A CFO ensures that your business scales strategically by aligning financial strategy with operational execution, mitigating risks, and optimizing financial resources. By leveraging forecasting, risk management tools like the risk matrix, and capital allocation strategies, a CFO empowers your company to scale effectively without unnecessary financial strain. For business owners, this means peace of mind, knowing that the financial foundation is secure, risks are proactively managed, and growth is pursued with a clear, strategic road map.

PREPARING TO SCALE

Before building your risk matrix, it's important to first get a clear view of everything that needs to happen operationally and strategically to prepare for growth. Follow these steps to create a focused and actionable scaling checklist:

Step 1 – Identify Core Areas to Prepare
Break your business down into key functional areas, such as:
1. **Operations** – Production capacity, supply chain readiness, inventory management
2. **Sales and Marketing** – Lead generation, sales processes, brand positioning
3. **Finance** – Funding needs, cash flow planning, financial controls
4. **Technology** – Platform scalability, IT infrastructure, cybersecurity
5. **People** – Hiring plans, leadership development, HR systems

Under each area, write down specific actions or upgrades needed to support growth. Be as detailed as possible; think "increase warehouse space by X sq. ft." not just "prepare operations."

Step 2 – Define Readiness Indicators
Scaling prematurely can be just as risky as scaling too late. Define the specific indicators that will tell you when you are ready to move forward by asking yourself:
1. What revenue or customer thresholds must we hit first?
2. What operational capacities must be secured (e.g., supplier

agreements, production throughput)?

3. What financial metrics (e.g., cash runway, profitability) must we achieve before scaling?

4. What leadership or staffing benchmarks must be met?

Next to each action item, note a clear milestone or condition that must be achieved before scaling.

Step 3 – Prioritize Your Checklist
Not all tasks are equally urgent. Rank your checklist items into three categories:

1. **Critical** – must be in place before scaling
2. **Important** – should be strengthened but not a blocker
3. **Nice to Have** – would help but not essential to start scaling

Step 4 – Assign Accountability
Scaling requires ownership. For each checklist item, assign a clear owner responsible for completing it. Use the name of one individual to ensure accountability; assigning multiple owners or a department may lead to items not being completed and finger-pointing.

Next to each task, write who is responsible and set a target completion date. By completing this checklist you will be laying out a solid foundation for the next phase of your company.

CHAPTER 14

YOU ARE SCALING YOUR COMPANY

When I was younger, I had a friend who started washing and detailing cars. It was just him and his cleaning supplies and equipment. He quickly gained a good reputation for his level of care and attention to detail and found himself running an incredibly busy and profitable operation. As with most small businesses, he had people in his ear asking when he was going to expand his business, take on employees, offer additional services, or reach other geographical areas. With his sights set on high revenue, he decided to expand, hiring employees, leasing commercial trucks to service other areas, and investing in more equipment.

Unfortunately, my friend learned quickly that while he was good at running a solo business, finding good employees, hiring, and managing their work was a very different story. He ran into issues with wasted product and broken equipment, and one of his vehicles was even in a traffic accident. His once 5-star business was now being flooded with lower reviews. He even had to stop taking a salary at one point to help cover the business's costs.

It's not that my friend was a bad business owner, but he scaled quickly and without a plan, which meant entering unfamiliar territory without the knowledge of how to do so. He got caught up in the potential of what his business could be, without paying attention to the risks. Had he brought on someone with the knowledge and skill set to guide him through growth, his business may have made it. In his situation, unfortunately, he ended up declaring bankruptcy and starting over with a new job.

I don't share this story to scare you if you're finding that your business is in the process of scaling organically. It's more of a cautionary tale of what can happen when we don't realize our blinds spots and don't bring in others with different skills who can help us grow. It makes me think of the quote that's often attributed to Benjamin Franklin, "An ounce of prevention is worth a pound of cure." Whereas Franklin was speaking about healthcare, I find it a relevant adage for scaling: When we prepare, we have a better chance of scaling in a healthy way.

But let's assume that you didn't plan for the growth that you're currently experiencing and are now trying to keep up and make the best decisions as you go. It is not too late to plan your scaling strategy— and a CFO might be the best person to help you do that!

EXECUTION OF SCALING

Think about how growth works in most areas of life. If you are trying to grow your muscles, you might follow a training regime to work out. If you are trying to grow your plants, you are going to water and fertilize them. If you're trying to grow the neural pathways of your brain, you might learn an instrument or a new language, or take a college course. We can grow in these ways, but we can also push growth too fast and cause harm. Over-training, over-watering, and over-studying often produce inverse results and stop growth in its tracks. The same can be true of businesses. The goal of scaling is to grow your company in a healthy and sustainable way, without breaking the company in the process.

What your company does will impact what your scaling process might look like. A beverage manufacturer, for example, might scale by leasing a larger warehouse space, purchasing more equipment, and hiring the employees needed to manage the increased operations. In this time, the beverage company might go from operating at maximum capacity to underutilizing its new equipment as they wait for more commercial accounts to start doing business with them. It means they have to plan for a period of consistent revenue, but significantly higher fixed and variable costs.

Conversely, a service-based business may find their growth constrained by the number of employees they have that can offer that service. Service-based businesses need to selectively hire new employees and onboard them appropriately to ensure that they are delivering the same level of quality service to customers. Finding the right person at the right time is challenging and may result in people being hired on, but having excess capacity in anticipation of customer growth. Relying on humans to drive revenue presents additional challenges due to the nature of human beings. People get sick, move, or take other positions, which can potentially throw a service-based business into a tailspin.

CFOS AND SCALING

As you can see, so much of scaling successfully is balancing the expenses you incur to grow with the financial resources you have available and the revenue you expect to receive. Scaling is a numbers game, and a CFO can provide much-needed oversight and management of the scaling project. A CEO is responsible for keeping business as usual going and creating the vision for the company in the future. A CEO must be kept aware of how the business is scaling, but ideally won't be directly involved with the actual scaling process. That is the value of a CFO. Having a CFO be in charge of your scaling means that they will be managing the outflow and inflow of capital, while also identifying risks before they become significant issues.

If you are already scaling and do not yet have a fractional or full-time CFO, now would be an ideal time to bring them in. If you've completed the checklist from the "Preparing to Scale" exercise, it can allow them to hit the ground running and get a handle on what's been done, what needs to be done, and how you plan to do it. Your CFO can help with the construction or evaluation of your risk matrix.

With a risk matrix in hand, your CFO will be able to more effectively monitor the scaling process. Because scaling is all about project management, they may also develop success criteria to ensure that the business is staying on top of their scaling plan. Leadership teams can apply KPIs and ratios to nearly any area of the business at any time to gather the data needed for informed decision-making.

Using these metrics, your CFO will be able to take corrective actions as needed to keep your scaling project on track. They will act as the trusted advisor of the CEO and leadership team, providing both awareness of the project's progress and solutions for challenges that arise. Imagine if you, the business owner, had this type of additional capacity to both keep your business running and watch it grow. Scaling with a CFO can make that happen.

CREATE YOUR RISK MATRIX

Every scaling company needs a risk matrix—even if you're already in the process of scaling. Your risk matrix can be created in a spreadsheet (my preference), a document using the table tool, or in programs like Power BI.

The matrix should have three categories: *Actions, Risks, and Issues*

Do the following:
1. Start by developing a comprehensive list of all actions associated with scaling your business
2. Identify any potential risks
3. Establish parameters for evaluating risk, like the probability of occurrence, the severity of impact, etc.
4. Assign a risk rating. I recommend a three-tiered scale such as Low Risk, Medium Risk, and High Risk
5. Create your risk matrix grid, with one axis as the probability of risk and the other axis as the severity of risk
6. Prioritize your risks. Now that you have a visual of what you're facing, decide which risks you want to address first
7. Create a plan to mitigate risks. Determine the actions you can proactively take to reduce your most severe and probably risks
8. If any of your risks do materialize and become issues, clearly identify them and assign all necessary resources to remediate such issues

Your risk matrix is something that you, your CFO, and your leadership team should refer back to often, ideally on a weekly basis. You can make adjustments as needed, but stay on top of managing your actions so risks do not arise and if they do, you proactively manage them so they do not materialize and become issues. The more you can prepare, the healthier your growth will be.

There is a great quote from a friend and coach when I was a competitive freediver that I have brought to this area of my professional life: "Train like you are competing and compete like you are training." In business, training becomes planning.

Risk Matrix - As of [Date]

Risk	Responsible	Mitigation Strategy	Probability (P)	Impact (I)	Risk Score	Priority
Describe the risk	Individual Name	What can be done to minimize the probability and/or impact of this risk	1 - Low 2 - Medium 3 - High	1 - Low 2 - Medium 3 - High	= (P) X (I)	Sort by Risk Score from High to Low
Risk # 1						
Risk # n						

		Probability (P)		
Risk		1	2	3
Impact (I)	1	1	2	3
	2	2	4	6
	3	3	6	9

CHAPTER 15

YOU ARE READY TO EXIT

The thought of exiting your business may be far from your mind, especially if you're a new startup. Some business owners don't want to hold on to their business forever. Serial entrepreneurs like myself enjoy the excitement of creating something new. That inevitably means at some point we will exit from our businesses, either due to a merger, an acquisition, or an IPO.

EXIT STRATEGIES

There are several common ways to exit a business in a profitable way. Each one strongly benefits from having a knowledgeable CFO as part of your executive leadership team, due to heavy requirements of providing financial information for buyers or investors to complete their due diligence process.

Merger

A merger is when two independent companies join together to form one new legal entity. Companies may decide to merge to expand their market share and customer reach, to horizontally integrate with a competitor or vertically integrate with another business in their supply chain, or for many other reasons. In a merger, there is a consolidation of the leadership team, almost inevitably involving top company management to exit the business. Most companies do not need two CEOs (and certainly not two CFOs!) at the helm.

Even if you plan not to be the one leading the company as a result of the merger, you want to make sure that you are leaving your assets and employees in a sound and stable environment. Your CFO can be the one to help vet the value added and the risks associated with the company you're merging with. They may be able to identify potential financial or cultural problems before the merger takes place. Having this information and being able to work on resolutions will ultimately lead you to a smoother transition.

Acquisition

Unlike a merger, during which a brand-new company is formed, an acquisition occurs when one company buys a controlling or full interest in another company while still retaining the acquiring company's identity. If your company is acquired, it becomes absorbed in the operations and structure of the acquiring parent company. Often in acquisitions, the leadership team of the acquired company is given a severance package to leave the organization. Some leaders may be retained in new roles or as consultants during a transition period. But before you can receive that nice payout, you need to find a business to acquire yours first.

A successful acquisition means maximizing the appeal of your company to potential buyers, while also managing and mitigating any risks that might be a turn-off for the deal. You should be looking to receive the best purchase price for your business, and your CFO can be the one to present your financials in the best possible light. Your CFO may also help you to negotiate the deal to ensure you're getting favorable terms in your purchase agreement and payout. There are also legal and regulatory requirements with mergers and acquisitions, and a CFO can be the one to help ensure that everything is filed properly and timely.

IPO and IPO Merger

Perhaps your future goals include taking your company public with an initial public offering (IPO). This is when a private company offers stock for purchase to the public for the first time to raise capital for the business.

IPOs are complicated and involve a tremendous amount of financial and legal paperwork. The process includes hiring investment banks and lawyers to help with registration. Then the company files a registration statement with the U.S. Securities and Exchange Commission (SEC). The investment bank then works to list the shares on a stock exchange for investors to buy and sell. A CFO is a necessary role to provide accurate and transparent financial reporting and to liaise with the many parties involved with the IPO.

There are also IPO mergers, in which a company will go public and raise capital. Once they have more cash, they will then merge with another company to increase their market share or expand their operations. This is an additionally complex situation that requires the financial expertise of a CFO, among other roles.

Reverse Merger or Reverse IPO

Perhaps your company has not gone public but has the desire to. There is a possibility that you could exit through what is known as a reverse merger or reverse IPO. In these situations, you will identify a public shell company (which is publicly traded but has no significant operations) to complete the process of going public. The private company's shareholders (your shareholders) acquire control of the public company by exchanging their private shares for public shares. The private company's management takes over the public company and continues operations under the private company's name. The result is that the once-private company is now public, bypassing the traditional IPO process.

Reverse mergers have the benefit over traditional IPOs in that they are faster and cheaper, avoiding the lengthy and expensive IPO process. There is also less regulatory scrutiny and no need for an SEC roadshow or traditional IPO underwriting. Reverse mergers allow private companies to gain the ability to raise capital as a publicly traded company and offer early investors and employees the opportunity to sell shares in the public market. The only major downside is the lack of rigorous vetting that would happen during a traditional IPO process, which might help identify if the shell company is low quality or has financial issues.

In reverse mergers, members of the leadership team of the public company may be offered a severance package to avoid duplicate leadership roles. As with the aforementioned situations, a CFO is a vital role to prepare for a reverse merger or reverse IPO. They will help to ensure that the transaction goes as smoothly as possible and that you are compensated fairly in the process.

PRESERVING THE INTEGRITY OF YOUR BUSINESS

During any transactions that involve the sale of ownership of your business, it is imperative that you have a strategic advisor to manage the sale while you continue to run the operations. I have unfortunately witnessed scenarios in which the CEO or leadership team of a company becomes so entrenched in the work of selling the business that the business breaks in the process. In those situations, the merger, acquisition, or IPO is then canceled, or worse, lawsuits become involved. You need to keep your business running smoothly while these exit activities are occurring. A CFO is the right person to manage that process.

Nearly all business merger, acquisition, and IPO arrangements require a thorough financial audit of at least two years of recent data. Having gone through several myself, I cannot overstate how extensive the audit process may be, requiring countless hours of providing supporting documentation to the audit teams. There are likely going to be additional reporting requirements to the SEC and other governing bodies if you're going through an IPO. The bandwidth needed to complete this work often stretches a leadership team to their limits.

If you are planning on any of these activities in the coming years, it is vitally important that you hire a CFO as soon as you are able. You and your leadership team need to remain committed and focused on overseeing employees and keeping the business operations running smoothly. Finding the right CFO to help you navigate through these challenges is not just a consideration—it is a necessity.

I challenge you to break out of the traditional mindset of what a CFO does to understand more of what they can do and how they can serve your business in the best way possible. When you are ready to exit, your CFO will be the one to support the transition so you can be on to your next business adventure!

THE CEO & CFO EXIT READINESS SIMULATION

The goal is to assess and refine the company's readiness for a potential exit by simulating key aspects of the process, including due diligence reviews, valuation assessments, and strategic positioning exercises. By proactively identifying gaps and opportunities before entering formal negotiations, the company can strengthen its market appeal, maximize its valuation, and navigate the exit process with greater confidence and control.

Step 1 – Define the Exit Strategy

CEO: Write a one-page summary outlining the ideal exit scenario (M&A, IPO, reverse merger). Include key reasons, timing, and what success looks like

CFO: Identify the financial metrics that must be optimized to make this exit attractive (e.g., revenue growth, EBITDA, margins, cash flow)

Step 2 – Conduct a Buyer/Investor Readiness Assessment

CEO & CFO Together:

1. Create a target acquirer/investor profile (Who would buy/invest in us and why?)
2. Identify three to five potential acquirers or investors
3. List potential concerns or red flags they might find

Step 3 – Perform a Due Diligence Stress Test

CEO:

1. Identify the top five questions an acquirer, investor, or underwriter would ask about strategy, market position, and risks

2. Identify key leadership, customer, or market risks that could impact valuation

CFO:

1. Prepare a "due diligence data room" checklist with financial statements, contracts, IP, HR, and tax compliance
2. Conduct an internal financial audit and stress test the company's valuation assumptions
3. Identify potential accounting issues or gaps

Step 4 – Valuation & Deal Scenario Planning
CEO & CFO Together:

1. Perform a valuation exercise using two to three different methods (discounted cash flow, revenue multiples, and/or precedent transactions)
2. Create a negotiation playbook (acceptable vs. non-negotiable terms)
3. Assess how much capital is needed (if IPO) or what synergies would attract a buyer (if M&A)

Step 5 – Simulate the Exit Pitch

CEO: Deliver a five-minute pitch to a mock buyer/ investor, articulating why the company is a valuable acquisition/IPO candidate

CFO: Defend the valuation, financials, and risk mitigation plan

Bonus: Invite a board member or external advisor to critique the exercise

By completing this exercise, the CEO and CFO will have a clearer road map to exit readiness, potential gaps to address, and a stronger strategic and financial narrative for potential buyers or investors.

CHAPTER 16

FINDING THE RIGHT CFO

I hope that this book has provided you with the clarity to know if and when you're ready for a CFO. Hiring a CFO is often a big financial undertaking, but if you have a strategy for when and how to bring one in, they can be tremendously helpful for your business. With enough growth, a CFO will become a necessity. Here are ways in which you can make sure you find the advisor that is right for you and your business.

THREE ASPECTS TO CONSIDER WHEN HIRING A CFO

It's time to discard any preconceived notions you may have about what skills make a good CFO. Let's instead start with a blank slate of expectations and build upon what I have found to be the most effective combination of skills for a CFO that can serve as your right-hand person.

1. Experience

There is no substitution for experience. The more businesses a CFO has worked with, either as a consultant, fractionally, or full-time, the more knowledgeable and resourceful they are likely to be for your business. They should demonstrate experience with financial reporting, budgeting, auditing, and analysis. Even more importantly, in my opinion, they should have leadership experience and illustrate how they've been able to inform strategy and contribute to the goals of their previous organizations.

If you find a CFO with leadership experience at a company either of your size or within your industry, that may be particularly valuable and their skill set may be well-paired with your organization. Many people are under the impression that a CFO should also be a CPA, but I find that belief has led to companies hiring the wrong person. Remember, the role and knowledge of an accountant is different than that of someone in finance. While a certified public accountant (CPA) license may be helpful for a CFO to have, it should not be a factor that weighs into your decision on who to hire. You likely already have CPAs on your accounting team to handle the technical side of transactions. Instead, focus on finding a CFO with industry-specific knowledge to help drive your company's goals forward.

2. Cultural Fit

Bringing in a CFO means you are including a key player whose approach to managing teams and driving change will impact most individuals in your business. It's important to make sure that they are a good fit for your company culture. In fact, a good fit is imperative. It doesn't matter how smart or experienced or credentialed a CFO is; if their approach to work is not compatible with the culture of your organization then they will never be a good fit.

One way you can assess this is by having your CFO applicants complete a personality assessment. This will give you a clearer picture of their management style, their strengths, and their weaknesses. You can also compare their assessment against your own to see if your styles are complementary or potentially at odds.

There are a few strategies to improve your odds of getting applicants who are a good cultural fit. The first is to incorporate your company values and aspects of your culture into the CFO job description. You may naturally select people who are more aligned with your culture and what you stand for. Secondly, you can collect references from former coworkers, who may be able to offer insights into the CFO candidate's working style, ethics, and ability to collaborate with others.

Culture questions can be a part of your interview process as well. Ask your candidates what their ideal work environment is like. Inquire as to how they manage stress, which is a given part of nearly every leadership position. You may even want to ask about what books they read or podcasts they listen to, to learn more about their interests and how well they might get along with others at your business.

3. Trust

Trust in your CFO is a crucial part of the role. But determining if someone is trustworthy during an interview process can be challenging. You can pay attention to their body language, facial expressions, and speech patterns during the interview and notice what your gut reaction is. Studies have found, however, that body language and eye contact are not necessarily reliable indicators of a person's truthfulness.

Instead, I have found it is more helpful to invite candidates to share times when they've made a mistake. Their willingness to admit to and own the mistake may indicate a person who is more willing to take responsibility for their actions, rather than trying to conceal any wrongdoing to appear perfect. It's also important to pay attention to the stories they share, both in and out of the interview, and how those line up against their resume.

If you are going to trust this person with your financial health, you want to make sure that you are confident in their ability to be honest, ethical, and trustworthy! This is most often what I see make or break a working relationship between a CEO and CFO.

CFO SKILLS TO LOOK FOR

A knowledge of finance is an obvious thing to look for in someone who is going to have the word as part of their job title. Being a talented CFO, though, is about so much more than having a financial background. You will be best served by a CFO that is a strategist and a planner—one who can take your vision and turn it into actionable steps with the financing to support it. A CFO with strong project management experience can be especially helpful because they are often well-versed at looking across the organization and understanding how multiple departments need to come together to drive results.

Your CFO must also have strong communication skills, as they are the face of your organization when it comes to working with investors, regulators, and boards. You want someone who is even-keeled under pressure and conservative in the information they share externally. You want a CFO that projects trust and integrity, and is willing to field financial questions with professionalism.

Lastly, your CFO should be able to demonstrate a strong work ethic. The role of CFO often requires many long hours, especially at the start of working with a company or when going through major business transactions like an acquisition or IPO. You want to know that your CFO is invested in getting the work done right and in a timely manner. This means being clearly focused on tasks and leading the accounting and finance teams by example. During the interview, ask questions that reveal how they perform under pressure and demonstrate commitment. For example:

1. "Can you tell me about a time when you faced a critical financial deadline and how you ensured everything was completed accurately and on time?"
2. "Describe a situation where you had to go above and beyond normal working hours or responsibilities to meet a major financial milestone. How did you manage your team through it?"

Look for answers that show not only technical competence but also leadership, prioritization skills, and a willingness to take ownership when it matters most. Ultimately, you would like to bring someone who is invested and excited for the success of your business.

HIRING YOUR FRACTIONAL CFO

The path to hiring your full-time CFO may be made easier if you've started with a fractional CFO and have been pleased with the work they've done. I have seen many fractional CFO roles turn into full-time hires for companies. If you have found that you are pleased with the work your fractional CFO has done, then you may wish to extend them an offer for full-time. Conversely, if you haven't been thrilled with the results that your fractional CFO has delivered, it's a good sign that you need to begin the process of finding a full-time CFO.

Unlike most other positions in an organization, a CFO is not a position that you want to have to fire and try hiring again if they don't work out. It's important to take your time and do your own due diligence to make sure your candidate seems like the right fit. Remember: The more planning and preparation you can do in advance, the more likely you'll be in achieving a successful result. Being planful in hiring a CFO is no different.

YOU ARE READY FOR A CFO

This is an exciting start on a new journey for your business. You hopefully now realize that a CFO is so much more than a number-cruncher and pencil-pusher. Your CFO will impact nearly all areas of your business, including existing partnerships. Having the right person, who can see things from different angles and work cross-functionally, will help you immensely as you grow. They will need people management skills, as they hold people accountable for meeting their numbers and explaining overages. They will need industry skills, as they analyze key ratios and compare them to your competitors. Most importantly, they will need to support you in your mission and vision. With support from the right CFO, your business can reach incredible heights.

UNDERSTANDING YOUR CFO'S PERSONALITY THROUGH THE ENNEAGRAM

In the beginning of this book, I recommended using the OCEAN personality test to build self-awareness as a business leader. Now, let's explore another powerful tool for understanding personality and motivations: the Enneagram.

The Enneagram identifies nine core personality types, each representing different ways people think, feel, and behave. It offers rich insights into strengths, leadership styles, communication tendencies, and even areas where individuals may struggle under pressure.

Unlike some frameworks, the Enneagram doesn't label any type as "good" or "bad." Every type brings unique value and every type faces its own set of challenges. Success comes not from picking the "right" number, but from understanding how your future CFO's natural tendencies will align with your company's needs.

Step 1 – Take the Enneagram Test Yourself
Start by experiencing the process firsthand.

1. Visit a reputable Enneagram site, such as The Enneagram Institute
2. Complete the test (typically takes ten to 15 minutes)
3. Review your primary Enneagram number and the associated core motivations, strengths, and potential growth areas
4. Reflect on whether your own results resonate with your leadership experiences and style

Step 2 – Have Your CFO Candidates Take the Test
Request that CFO candidates complete the same Enneagram test as part of the hiring process and ask them to share their top two Enneagram numbers and the accompanying description.

Emphasize that there are no wrong answers; this exercise is about self-awareness and team fit, not judgment.

Step 3 – Analyze the Insights Thoughtfully
Once you have the candidate's Enneagram type, reflect on:

1. **Strengths** – What leadership qualities or working styles does this type naturally bring? (Example: Type 1s are highly principled and detail-oriented; Type 8s are decisive and assertive leaders)
2. **Challenges** – Where might this person experience stress or blind spots in a CFO role? (Example: A Type 6 may excel in risk management but need reassurance during high-ambiguity periods)
3. **Team Dynamics** – How might this person's type complement or clash with your leadership style?

Write a few notes about how this candidate's personality might fit into your company's culture and leadership team dynamics.

Please remember that the Enneagram isn't about making or breaking a candidate's chances; it's about deepening your understanding of how they will lead, collaborate, and grow alongside you as your business scales.

CONCLUSION

It's very easy to get lost if you don't know where you're going.

When I was a university student, my labor economics professor, Dr. Hoke, assigned a project that would end up altering the course of my life. He called it "The Personal Plan." Its intent was quite simple. In a class about labor economics, he wanted us to identify how we fit in the labor market when we graduated. On a deeper level, the project was to help us know ourselves better. The professor's hope was that in getting clear on our vision we would be able to clearly articulate it in the future to potential employers.

It started with crafting our personal mission and personal vision for life. We had to document and explore our personal values, like what type of work we were willing to do and what we were not willing to do. There was a SWOT analysis component to evaluate ourselves based on our strengths, weaknesses, opportunities, and threats. We worked on this over the course of the semester and by the end we had prepared a very nice document.

When my dad passed away in the fall of 2023, I was in the early stages of planning my current company. At that time, I returned to our family home in Spain to help with the cleanup. There, tucked safely away, I found a document I had written back in college. I knew it was there, but I could barely remember what I had written all those years ago. Sitting on my bed, surrounded by boxes filled with memories (notebooks, greeting cards, ideas scribbled on napkins), I opened the document.

As I began reading, I was both shocked and pleasantly surprised by my plan. Despite the many directions my life had taken since college (the ups, downs, and unexpected curveballs), the vision and values I had written more than two and a half decades earlier still rang true. It turns out, the personal goals I outlined then are still guiding my life today. Some of those goals remain works in progress (I'm still working hard toward buying that dream boat!), but I have been fortunate enough to achieve the ones that mattered most.

I married a remarkable woman, Marcelle, and we have the two most amazing children in the world (though I won't argue if you say the same about yours!), Sofi and Nico. And just as I had hoped decades before they were born, I now wake up every day with the mission to be as present a father as I can be. I attend all their events, do their homework with them, coach them for their sports, and participate in their bedtime routines, even if it means staying up into the early hours of the morning afterward to catch up on my work. No matter how busy life gets, nothing comes before my family.

I knew back in college that I wanted to work very hard early on in my career. I did this because I also knew that eventually I wanted to get married and have kids, and that my family would become my priority. I still work very hard and hold my work in high regard, but there's rarely a day that goes by when I don't sit with them at breakfast, or a night when I don't give them a bath or read them to sleep. The most important thing in my life right now is being a present dad, because

I believe strongly that the work we do for our children in these early, formative years shapes them for the rest of their lives.

While the Personal Plan exercise is not directly related to the topic of this book on determining when a CFO is right for you, I have decided to include instructions for it here for you to try yourself. I imagine that if we as entrepreneurs are similar in personality, then you too may have a curiosity of what your plan would look like. Now that I am a university professor myself, I give this assignment to every one of my students. It can teach us valuable lessons—not just for business, but for life.

WHAT DRIVES ME FORWARD

My mission since that project has always been the same: use the skills that I have to help people who need them. This vision has informed the work I do today with my new healthcare company and focusing on the needs of underserved children. I want to use my business to help others gain the care they need. Once they have their health, they are better equipped to learn. The more they can learn, the more successful they may be in their future careers. The more successful they can be in their careers, the more they can serve their families and communities and break the cycle of poverty.

I am always looking for new and impactful ways to give back. It's really hard for me to see companies failing. It bothers me to see companies that are doing okay but could be doing so much better. I know that if businesses had the right tools and knowledge, they could be so much further ahead. Knowing how to do things is a game changer, but sometimes it seems that knowledge is hoarded among a relatively small community who knows the formula to make each other rich, but doesn't share that formula with the world. I want to end the knowledge gap. Sharing my expertise from years of working in the field of finance, economics, and entrepreneurship became a new goal for me. It was my motivation for writing this book. I want you to succeed. You deserve to know the strategies and steps that have helped other successful businesses thrive.

But the limit with this book is that I can only share what I know. Then it becomes up to you to take action. Taking action means scheduling time to step back and assess yourself and your business. It means having tough financial conversations and changing how you work. It may mean cutting back your spending in ways you haven't before, with the goal of aligning your business with what truly matters to you.

BEYOND FORMAL EDUCATION

Let this book serve as your reminder to return to common sense. We live in a world that is overflown with information that is easily available to us, but it's not all good information and it can be exhausting to sort through for the truth. I still believe in the importance of gut feelings and using industry benchmarks for your company size to determine if the decisions you are making pass the commonsense rules.

Remember what I mentioned about common sense at the beginning of this book? From my youth, my metric has been, "Was I doing something that my parents or grandparents would approve of?" As a business leader, I ask myself that question when it comes to spending and being transparent with company leaders and investors about it. If I don't feel comfortable explaining it to the people to whom I am accountable, then it's probably not a good purchase.

Chances are you are a business leader because you have a gut instinct that has led you there. You had a hunch that the goods or services you provide were needed in the market. You created your MVP and found your customers. You may have achieved part of this because of the education you had, but I believe an even greater part of entrepreneurship and business management comes from something inside. It's who you are as a person.

Though this book has come to an end, I hope that this is just the start for you on a new journey forward. I hope that you feel more focused or empowered on what your business may be able to achieve. You may even be dreaming of your company's exit strategy for the first time in your professional life!

I hope that this book becomes a well-worn resource for you, one that you return to at each stage of growth in your business to remind yourself of some of the key rules to spending, saving, and scaling. I hope that you continue to build your confidence in your financial knowledge and how ratios and KPIs can be used to drive the best data based decisions. In the future, I would love to see communities of entrepreneurs who have read this book come together to support each other and challenge each other to complete the exercises in each chapter. This book could be the first step of an entrepreneurial movement.

My curious children, knowing how much time I have poured into creating this book, asked me what it is about. I explained to them that it is about being clear on your purpose and making decisions that feel aligned with it. I told them the book is about knowing ourselves and knowing when and how to lean on others for support. I shared that it is about being respectful of our money and allocating it accordingly. My daughter, Sofi, looked pensive for a moment and then exclaimed, "You should call the book *Make Good Choices!*"

It was a proud parenting moment for me, seeing that she could recognize, even at a young age, that so much of the direction and momentum in our lives can come down to our choices, even the ones that are difficult or uncomfortable to make. I hope that this book has inspired you in that way and that you feel more empowered in the running of your business.

What I really hope most of all is the same wish I have for my kids: that you never stop learning. You may have had barriers in your past, but you have the ability to blaze a trail into a new and better future. You may have experienced entrepreneurial setbacks in the past, but now you are a new person, with new information, to approach your business endeavors in a new way. I want you to reach the point where you need a fractional CFO and then a full-time CFO. I want that to be part of your vision and now feel within reach.

What is your mission? What do you want to give to the world? Take the tools you have learned here and figure out a way to do it. Know that I am here cheering you on!

APPENDIX

The Personal Plan Assignment

Create a free-format document including the following sections:

Mission

- To Self
- To Family
- To Employer

Mechanisms for Success

- Always - What are things you always promise to do (e.g., Exercise regularly, tend to your relationships/friendships, etc.)
- Never - What are things you would never do (e.g., Knowingly harm another person, steal, etc.)

Goals

- Short Term
- Lifetime

SWOT Analysis

- Strengths
- Weaknesses
- Opportunities
- Threats

Define Success

- Personal Success
- Professional Success

ACKNOWLEDGMENTS

Writing this book has been a journey of passion, perseverance, and collaboration, and I am deeply grateful to the many people who made it possible.

First, my heartfelt thanks to my family for their unwavering love and support. Special thanks to Sofi and Nico for their creativity and input with the title and cover respectively!

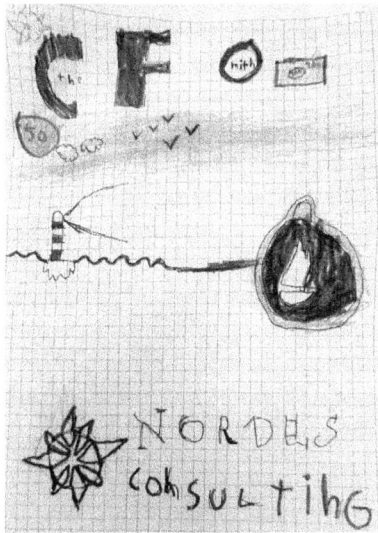

To my teachers, mentors, and colleagues who have taught me some of the valuable lessons that have shaped this book.

Infinite gratitude to Amber Vilhauer for encouraging me on this journey.

To the team at KN Literary Arts for their guidance and support all along the way, thank you, I couldn't have done it without you, especially Jillian Abby.

Finally, to my readers: Thank you for picking up this book. Your support makes this dream a reality, and I truly hope that this book helps you in your personal and professional journey.

With gratitude,
Rodrigo

ABOUT THE AUTHOR

Rodrigo Rodríguez-Novás is the CEO of NORDES Consulting and a seasoned expert in global finance, strategy, and M&A. An MBA graduate and business school professor, he helps leaders navigate complexity with clarity and purpose. A former competitive freediver, Rodrigo brings the same calm focus and discipline to the boardroom that he once brought to the depths of the ocean

www.ingramcontent.com/pod-product-compliance
Lightning Source LLC
Chambersburg PA
CBHW030511210326
41597CB00013B/864